HOW TO WRITE IMPRESSIVE BUSINESS LETTERS

GOODWILL'S

HOW TO WRITE
IMPRESSIVE BUSINESS LETTERS

JENS NELSON

Published by :

GOODWILL PUBLISHING HOUSE
B-9, Rattan Jyoti, 18,
Rajendra Place, New Delhi-110 008

Price : Rs. 75

Published by :
GOODWILL PUBLISHING HOUSE
B-9, Rattan Jyoti, 18, Rajendra Place,
New Delhi-110 008, (INDIA)
Phone : 5750801

Printed at :
Star Offset Printers, New Delhi.

CONTENTS

1.	*OFFICE PREMISES*	*14–27*
1.	Letter to a Property Dealer for a Showroom	15
2.	Letter to a Property Dealer for Suitable Flat on Rent	16
3.	Reply to the above	17
4.	Letter for Taking-over Office Premises on Lease	18
5.	An Advertisement for Business Premises	19
6.	An Advertisement for Sale of Residential Apartment	20
7.	Letter in Response to an Advertisement for Business Premises	21
8.	Letter Asking Repairs	22
9.	Letter Requesting Renewal of Lease	23
10.	Letter Remitting Rent of an Office Premises	24
11.	Letter Requesting Estimate of Decoration of Premises	25
12.	Letter Requesting Time for Payment of Rent	26
13.	Reply to the above Granting Time to Pay Rent	27

2.	*ENQUIRIES, REPLIES AND QUOTATIONS*	*28–42*
1.	Letter of Enquiry about Trade-terms	29
2.	Reply to the above	30
3.	Letter from an Individual Customer Enquiring about Kitchen-installation	32
4.	Letter Requesting for Catalogue and Price-list	33
5.	Reply to the above	34
6.	Letter of Enquiry about Carpets etc.	35
7.	Reply to the above.	36
8.	Letter Asking Goods on Approval	37
9.	Letter Requesting Quotation for Crockery	39
10.	Enquiry about Books on Sale or Return Basis	40
11.	A Buyer's Letter Requesting Better Terms	41
12.	Reply to the above	42
3.	*ORDERS AND THEIR EXECUTION*	*43–63*
1.	Order for Cordless Telephone and Receive-Amplifier	45
2.	Acknowledgement of the above	46
3.	Order for a Watch from an Individual Customer	47
4.	Reply to the above	48
5.	Letter Placing an Order	49
6.	Letter Regretting Delay in Supply	50
7.	Follow-up Letter as the Order is Incomplete	51
8.	Letter Notifying Partial Extention of an Order	53

9.	Letter Notifying Delay in the Execution of an Order	54
10.	Letter Showing Inability to Execute an Order	56
11.	Letter Notifying Cancellation of an Order	58
12.	Reply to the above	59
13.	Letter from a Buyer Regretting Delay in Executing an Order	60
14.	Letter Acknowledging the Receipt of Goods	61
15.	Letter Notifying the Execution of an Order	62
16.	Letter Requesting for Forwarding Instructions.	63
4.	*COMPLAINTS AND ADJUSTMENTS*	*64–78*
1.	Complaints about Defective Goods	66
2.	Complaint about Unsatisfactory Service of a Washing Machine	67
3.	Reply to the above Complaint	68
4.	Complaint about Non-delivery of Goods	69
5.	Reply to the above	70
6.	Complaint about Goods received in Excess	71
7.	Complaint Regarding Receipt of Wrong Goods	72
8.	Reply to the above	73
9.	Complaint about Wrong Statement	74
10.	Reply to the above Complaint	75
11.	Letter in Response to a Complaint about a Defective Carpet	76

12.	Complaint about Goods Received in Damaged Condition	77
13.	Buyer's Complaint about Delivery Charges	78
5. STATUS AND TRADE REFERENCES		***79–94***
1.	The Buyer's Request to Supply Goods on Credit	81
2.	Supplier's Favourable Reply (I)	82
3.	Supplier's Unfavourable Reply	83
4.	The Supplier Asking for References	84
5.	The Buyer Supplies Business References	85
6.	The Supplier takes-up Reference with a Trader	86
7.	Trader's Favourable Response	87
8.	Trader's Qualified Reference	88
9.	Trader's Unfavourable Reference	89
10.	Bank's Favourable Reply	90
11.	Bank's unfavourable Reply	91
12.	Agency's Favourable Reply	92
13.	Agency's Unfavourable Reply	93
14.	Supplier's Favourable Response (II)	94
6. COLLECTION LETTERS		***95–111***
1.	Supplier's Request for Payment	96
2.	First Reminder for Payment	97
3.	Second Reminder for Payment	98
4.	Third Reminder for Payment	99
5.	The Buyer Promises to Pay	100

6. Buyer Explains Inability to Settle the Account 101

7. Buyer Sends a Part-Payment 102

8. Supplier's Reply to the above 103

9. Buyer Settles the Account 104

10. Buyer's Request to an Individual Customer for Payment 105

11. The Customer Replies 106

12. Supplier Suggests Payment in Instalments 107

13. Supplier Returns the Excess Amount 108

14. Supplier Offer Special Discour.t on Bill 109

15. Customer Sends the Bill for Correction 110

16. Reply to the above 111

7. CIRCULAR AND NOTICES *112–116*

1. Circular Notifying Opening of a New Branch 113

2. Circular about Clearance Sale 114

3. Circular Introducing a New Sales Representative 115

4. Circular Announcing a New Partner 116

8. GOODWILL LETTERS *117–124*

1. Congratulations on Moving to a Better and More Spacious Office-space 118

2. Letter of Condolence on the Death of an Employee 119

3. Letter of Condolence to a Buyer 120

4. Letter of Sympathy to a Business-friend 121

5. Letter Regretting Price-increase 122

6. Letter of Thanks for Prompt Execution of an Order 123

7. Letter of Thanks for First Order 124

9. *AGENTS AND AGENCIES*	*125–131*

1. Letter Applying for an Agency 126
2. Letter Offering Agency Rights 127
3. Acceptance of Sole Agency 128
4. Agent's Request for Increase in Commission 129
5. Letter Declining to Raise Commission 130
6. Conditional Acceptance of an Offer for Agency 131

10. *BANKING CORRESPONDENCE*	*132–142*

1. Letter to a Bank to Open a Current Account 133
2. Letter Requesting to stop Payment of a Cheque 134
3. Letter to Bank Claiming Balance in the Account of a Deceased Customer 135
4. Reply to the Claimant for transferring the Balance to his Account 136
5. Letter Reporting the Loss of a Locker's Key 137
6. Letter to Bank Requesting Overdraft Facility 138
7. Reply to the above 139
8. Letter Informing a Customer about Expiry of an Overdraft Facility 140
9. Letter to a Customer Regarding Maintaining Minimum Balance in the Account 141

10. Letter Allowing Overdraft Facility to a Customer 142

11. *INSURANCE CORRESPONDENCE* 143–151

1. Letter Asking Insurance Rates 144
2. Letter Asking for Life Insurance Cover 145
3. Reply to the above 146
4. Follow-up Letter Accepting Insurance 147
5. Letter to an Insurance Company Seeking Information about Surrender Value of a Policy 148
6. Letter to an Insurance Company for Settling Claims on Husband's Death 149
7. Letter to an Insurance Company about Increase in Cover 150
8. Letter to an Insurance Company about Tour Insurance 151

12. *APPLICATION FOR APPOINTMENTS* 152–182

1. Application for the Post of an Accounts Clerk 154
2. Application for the Post of a Medical Representative 156
3. Application for the Post of a Typist Clerk 158
4. Application for the Post of a Counter Sales-girl 159
5. Application for the Post of a Lady Telephone Operator 160
6. Application for the Post of a Food Technologist 161
7. Application for the Post of a Steno Typist 162

8. Application for the Post of Manager Bulk Drugs 163
9. Application for the Post of an Accounts Officer 164
10. Application for the Post of Private Secretary 165
11. Application for the Post of a Sales Organizer 167
12. Application for the Post of a Trading Manager 168
13. Letter Taking up a Reference 170
14. A Favourable Reply to the above 172
15. Another Letter Requesting a Reference 173
16. A Letter of Recommendation 174
17. Another Letter of Recommendation 175
18. A Testimonial 176
19. Letter of Thanks to a Referee 177
20. A Letter Inviting for an Interview 178
21. Letter Confirming Attendance for Interview 179
22. An Appointment Letter 180
23. Letter Accepting the Employment 181
24. Letter Declining an Employment 182

13. TRAVEL TOURS AND HOTELS *183–192*

1. Enquiry about Fares etc. 184
2. Letter Requesting Hotel Reservation 185
3. Letter Enquiring about Hotel Accommodation 186
4. Reply to the above 187

5. Another Letter Seeking Hotel Reservation 188

6. Reply to the Above 189

7. Letter to a Travel Agent for Arranging a Business Trip 190

8. Letter Chartering a Tourist Bus 191

9. Letter about Seminar Facility in a Hotel 192

14. RAIL, ROAD AND SEA TRANSPORT 193–202

1. Complaint to the Railway Authorities 194

2. Notifying Despatch of Goods by Railway Parcel 195

3. Letter to Railway Authorities Requesting Redirections of Consignment 196

4. Enquiry about Freight and Sailing Schedule 197

5. Asking the Agent to Collect Consignment for Shipping 198

6. Agent's Reply to the above 199

7. Letter Asking Freight Rates from a Transport Operator 200

8. Letter Asking Quotation for Transportation of Office Equipment etc. 201

9. A Circular from a Transporter 202

15. COMMERCIAL TERMINOLOGY 203–224

16. COMMERCIAL ABBREVIATIONS 225–234

17. WORDS COMMONLY CONFUSED 235–240

18. WORDS COMMONLY MISSPELT 241–261

ONE

OFFICE PREMISES

An office is a place from where business or work, that is administrative, clerical, professional etc. is carried on. Thus, an office premises plays an important role in running any service, business or profession. It is the hub of the business activity. It is a must for each and every establishment, business-house, factory or firm where it can house its office. It occupies the same position in a business as does the mind in the human body.

You may have a small office initially, but with the expansion of business you may find your present accommodation insufficient and so you may like to shift to better and more spacious location. Then you may like to take over on existing premises on lease from the previous occupants at a premium. In that case the outgoing company may sell you the lease.

An office premises should be such which can meet all your office requirements, and suitably be located and easily accessible. For the success of any business it is imperative that the office accommodation is selected with proper planning and thinking. This involves a lot of correspondence and negotiation. Sometimes, it may be done by your lawyer or legal advisor, but on many an occassion you may be required to write your own letters individually in this matter.

1. Letter to a Property Dealer for a Showroom

GOOD TIME (M) SDN BHD
Kompleks Nagaria
Kuala Lumpur

27th May, 19... Telephone : 03-293 8886

The Manager
United Property Consultants Sdn. Bhd.
Wisma Equity
Kuala Lumpur

Dear Mr. Cheong Wing Chan

We are authorized dealer for exclusive branded watches, pens, lighters, clocks, calculators etc. We already have our main showroom at the above address. But we are interested in opening another one in Mui Plaza, Jalan P. Ramlee, Kuala Lumpur. The showroom should be approximately of 2000 square feet on the ground floor. It should be airconditioned, well-furnished, and with fax, telex and mail message services.

We may tell you that we require this showroom at the earliest quite urgently. For us the rent is immaterial, what we want is a premises ideally located with all the above facilities. We may also consider an offer of outright purchase.

We look forward to your immediate response so that the premises may be seen and terms and conditions settled at an early date.

Yours sincerely

Tai Whatt

2. *Letter to a Property Dealer for Suitable Flat on Rent for an Executive.*

ABC INSURANCE BROKERS SDN BHD
Amoda Building, Jalan Imbi
Kuala Lumpur

16 June, 19...   Telephone : 03-2418121

The Manager
Mainland Properties Sdn. Bhd.
Wisma Tek Lee
Kuala Lumpur

Dear Mr. Hashim

We urgently require a ready built two bedroom delux suite of 1000 square feet covered area for our Chief Executive Officer on rent. It should be in any posh locality and within 20 kilometers from our office and preferably facing a park. It can be on 3rd or 4th floor with proper parking, security and lift facilities.

The flat should be well-furnished and decorated. We are prepared to pay reasonable advance and security deposit.

We would like to hear from you soon.

Yours faithfully

K. Teng San
Manager

3. *Reply to the above*

MAINLAND PROPERTIES SDN BHD
Wisma Tek Lee, Kuala Lumpur

21 June, 19... Telephone : 03-229 4726

The Manager
ABC Insurance Borkers Sdn. Bhd.
Amoda Building, Jalan Imbi
Kuala Lumpur

Dear Mr. K. Teng San

We thank you for your letter of 16th June, 19... regarding a ready to move in deluxe suite for your Chief Executive Officer on rent lease.

We are glad to say that we have a couple of deluxe suites in the area of your choice. They have all the facilities you want. They are well furnished, decorated and with car parking and 24 hours security facilities. They all have lift facilities as well.

One of these suites is two side open on the third floor and faces a large public park. The windows are large, commanding panoramic view of the surroundings. In my opinion it will suit you best. Moreover, the rent is reasonable and the advance and security deposit being asked is also reasonable.

We can show you this suite any day at your convenience, but you should be quick as we are receiving a few more enquiries about this particular flat and we would not like you to be disappointed. We can also show you other suitable deluxe suites in posh localities if you so desire.

You may send your representative immediately so that the matter may be further discussed and the suite shown to him.

Yours sincerely

A. Hashim

4. *Letter for Taking-Over Office Premises on Lease*

ICEMAN (M) SDN BHD
Pandan Jaya, Cheras Kuala Lumpur

Telephone : 03-986 1771
Fax : 03-985 5233

The Manager
Kam Swee Sdn. Bhd.
B-61, Jalan Kepong
Kuala Lumpur

Dear Sir

We are very much interested in taking from you your existing lease with regard to the above premises for our branch office. In this regard we would like to have this premises inspected by our representative soon, but at your convenience. We would also like to have a look at the existing lease and other relevant documents before further discussions in the matter.

We would like to refurnish and redecorate the premises to suit our liking, however, we would like to purchase from you the existing telephone, telex and fax facilities.

We look forward to your early response so that the premises and its legal documents can be seen and premium etc. can be decided in the immediate future.

Yours faithfully

Chong Fook Peng
General Manager

5. *An Advertisement for Business Premises*

FURNISHED A.C. CABINS WITH
FAX/TELEX/MAIL MESSAGE SERVICES

Near Export Trade Centre
Kuala Lumpur

CONTACT IMMEDIATELY
UNIVERSAL BUSINESS CENTRE
NO. 21, JALAN YEW, PUDU
KUALA LUMPUR, Fax-03-984 1616

6. *An Advertisement for Sale of Residential Apartment*

OPPORTUNITY IN SINGAPORE
FOR
MULTI-NATIONALS, DIAMOND/PEARL &
JEWELLERY TRADERS.

FOR SALE

Large Three Bedroom Appartment
2500 Sq. Ft.) Complete Floor,
central location,
(Apartment Facing Park with
Panoramic View of the City)

APPLY to BOX NO. 299 cs,
BUSINESS INDONESIA, 1 SOPHIA ROAD,
26 PEACE CENTRE, SINGAPORE

No Brokers Please.

7. *Letter in Response to an Advertisment for Business Premises.*

Room No. 103
Amra Hotel
165, Tanjong Pagar Road
Singapore

12 November, 19...

The Advertisor
Box No. 65733
The Asian Wall Street Journal
6, Battery Road
Singapore

Dear Sir

I am interested in taking over on lease the business premises with A.C. telephone and fax facilities advertised in today's *Asian Wall Street Journal.*

In this regard I would like to have specific details in connection with area of space, floor and the rent per square foot and advance amount etc. before further negotiations can be held. I would like to come and see the premises personally at the earliest.

Actually I want ready to move in office premises. Therefore, the accommodation should be already well furnished and decorated. Our requirement is 100-150 sq. mts. inclusive of W.C., and a kitchenette and parking facility for 3-4 cars. It should be preferably on the ground floor or the first floor.

I look forward to your prompt response and details as I want the office premises on urgent basis.

Yours faithfully

Munis Raza

8. *Letter Asking Repairs*

Edwin Dental Clinic
21, Upper Thomson Road
Singapore

20 June, 19...

Mr. Lim Soh Liang
22, Beach Road
Singapore

Dear Mr. Liang

I have been in possession of the above premises for the last ten years, where I have been running my dental clinic. This accommodation has been with me on lease. As you are aware some urgent repairs were carried out three years back though as per our lease agreement, I am entitled for repairs and white-washing every year. As far minor repairs are concerned, I have never bothered you and got them done at my own expense. But now the premises needs some urgent repairs including whitewash, painting of doors and wooden fixtures and replacement of W.C. and electric wirings.

I shall be grateful if you come yourself or send your agent immediately so that the repairs may be carried out in near future. At present it is almost in a dilapidated condition as I feel much inconvenience and my business is adversely affected. Moreover, I would like that these repairs are carried out on Sundays only when the clinic is closed for customers and clients.

During all these years of my possession of the above premises I have been very particular in payment of rents in time. I also increased the rent to your full satisfaction at the time of renewal of the lease every time. As such our relations as a tenant and landlord have been very healthy and cordial. I, therefore, look forward to your immediate action in the matter.

Yours faithfully,

(Dr.) Sin Ah Kauh

9. *Letter Requesting Renewal of Lease*

BABY COMFORTS CORPN SDN BHD
15, Jalan Mewah Cheras
Kuala Lumpur

10, July 19...

Tel : 03-931 5988
03-931 8185

Mr. Heng Chan Hup
191, Jalan Amunuddin Baki
Kuala Lumpur

Dear Mr. Hup

Subject : Regarding renewal of lease
15, Jalan Mewah Cheras, Kuala Lumpur

As you are well aware, the lease of the above premises in our possession expires on 31st August, 19... as per the terms and conditions of the lease and rent-agreement. As we want to continue our business from this place, we request you to extend the lease for further period of 7 years with effect from 1st September 19... at the same terms and conditions.

In view of the higher maintenance cost, rise in prices and increased rates of taxes on commercial property, we are ready to increase the present rent by 35% which, I hope, would satisfy you.

We look forward to your early reply and action in the matter so that a new lease agreement can be executed in time before the expiry of the present one.

With thanks

Yours sincerely

Vivian Smith
Manager

10. Letter Remitting Rent of an Office Premises

DATA SCAN PTE LTD
Off. Bukit Timah Road
27-B, Duchess Street
Singapore

2, April, 19... Telephone : 467 7788

Mr. Bernard Lee
21, Beach Road
Singapore

Dear Mr. Lee

We are pleased to enclose in advance a bunch of six cheques nos. 00071245 to 00071250 each for Singapore $2500 towards rent for the above office premises in our possession and use. The cheques are crossed and drawn in your favour and on Pt. Bank, Negaria, Indonesia, Dapenso Building, 158 Cecil Street Singapore Branch.

These six post dated cheques are towards rent for the months of May to October, 19... Please acknowledge receipt of the above cheques by signing and returning the enclosed voucher for our record.

With thanks

Yours sincerely

Mohmmad Ali
Manager Finance

11. Letter Requesting Estimate of Decoration of Premises

SUPREME AUTO PTE LTD
Upper Aljunied Lane
Singapore

21 March, 19... Telephone : 286 3978
289 6775

The Manager
Aradia Furnishing Pte. Ltd.
Watten Rise
Singapore

Dear Sir

We are interested in getting our ground floor office premises at the above location re-furnished and decorated.

The net floor area to be furnished and decorated is about 1500 sq. feet. We would like to have carpeted it from wall to wall.

We want contemporary solid wood furniture for our personnel use besides some synthetic resin chairs for our customers and clients. We also want state-of-the-art technique lighting fixtures for our present office.

We would appreciate if you send your representative to see our office premises with provisional estimates, samples, catalogue etc. We want to get the decoration work done as early as possible.

We look forward to an early visit by your representative.

Yours faithfully

G.B. Goh
Manager

12. *Letter Requesting Time for Payment of Rent*

Noval Hairdressing Salon
Jalan Besar, Keppong
Kuala Lumpur.

10 May, 19... Telephone : 0364 4263

Mr. Anwar Ali
40 Jalan Sultan Ismail
Kuala Lumpur

Dear Mr. Ali

As you are aware, I was involved in an accident necessitating my hospitalisation and treatment for about 2 months. During this period my saloon remained closed and there was no business. Moreover, I had to pay for my hospitilisation and such other expenses. As a result of this unforseen turn of events, I am totally unable to pay the rent for the current and the following months.

I am the only earning member in our family of seven members, and this has made my financial position all the more bad.

I shall, therefore, be grateful if you allow me to delay the payments, of rent for these two months of May and June until the beginning of July when I expect to be in a position to fulfil my financial commitments.

I hope you would appreciate my difficulties and allow me this period to pay you the rent in lump sum for three months in the month of July.

With thanks and best wishes.

Yours faithfully

Sun Loh Mah

13. *Reply to the above Granting Time to Pay Rent*

40 Jalan Sultan Ismail
Kuala Lumpur

21 May, 19...

Mr. Sun Loh Mah
Novel Hairdressing Salon
Jalan Besar, Keppong
Kuala Lumpur

Dear Mr. Mah

I really feel sorry for your financial difficulties arising out of your unfortunate accident and subsequent hospitalisation etc. I fully sympathise with you and wish all the best.

I am willing to grant you the time requested to pay the rent in lump sum for three months in the beginning of the month of July. In your adverse circumstances I cannot think of pressing you to pay me the rent immediately as you have always been punctual in paying your rent all these years.

I hope your financial and other problems are temporary and you would soon overcome these as you are back to your salon and work.

Yours faithfully

Anwar Ali

TWO

ENQUIRIES, REPLIES AND QUOTATIONS

An enquiry may be defined as a request seeking information regarding prices, quotations, estimates, terms and conditions of business and such other related matters. Though Enquiries and their Replies etc. fall under routine business correspondence yet they form an integral and important part of any business activity for many significiant reasons.

The importance of enquiries should never be underestimated as they are from prospective buyers. As such, they should not be treated casually. They should be attended promptly and carefully in order to turn them into sure orders for your goods or services. Enquiries and responses to them should always be result-oriented. And so they should be brief, clear, exact, simple, direct and prompt. You should be very precise about what information you seek and from whom.

Enquiries should be dealt with promptly and courteously for boosting your business and creating goodwill. They can be transformed into sales, profits and lot of goodwill if handled properly and imaginatively. They should always be replied into 'thank you style'. Try to satisfy your customer as best as you can be being quick in your replies containing the information requested. Give exact information in clear, precise and simple terms always keeping in mind that "Customer is a King".

1. *Letter of Enquiry about Trade-terms*

FAIRDEAL FURNITURE CO.
Block 48, Toa Payoh
Singapore

12 January, 19...

Telephone : 353 40114
Fax : 259 3671

The Manager
IL & D Converters Pte. Ltd.
Lorong Tukang Tiga
Singapore

Dear Sir

We deal in a wide range of quality furniture. We also supply these items on rent on very reasonable rates and so have a vast clientele in Singapore, Malaysia and Indonesia.

Recently we saw your advertisements in newspapers and also on T.V. regarding your fibre glass furniture suitable for all weather. We are interested in it since we have received several enquiries of late about these items of outdoor and indoor leisure and fashionable furniture.

We would feel obliged if you send your representative immediately with your trade terms, payment condition and catalogues so that the matter may be settled at the earliest. We can assure you of repeat bulk orders for your cool-cane furniture items made of glass fibres if your terms and conditions are found favourable and satisfying in regard to commission and payment schedule.

We look forward to your prompt response and action in the matter.

Yours faithfully

Martin Lee
General Manager

2. *Reply to the above*

I & D CONVERTERS PTE LTD
Lorong Tukang Tiga
Singapore

20 January 19... Telephone: 266 3121

The General Manager
Fairdeal Furniture & Co.
Block 48, Toe Payoh
Singapore

Dear Mr. Lee

We are in receipt of your letter of enquiry of 12th January regarding our fibre glass furniture. We thank you for your keen interest in our items of leisure outdoor/indoor furniture made of glass fibres.

In this regard we are pleased to inform you that our furniture is very popular as it brings that best of the two words: cane-looking but without the undesirable qualities of cane wood. It is rust-free, fade-free, easily washable and light in weight. Moreover, it does not have any loose ends or sharp nails. There are many attractive colours and designs to choose from to suit your taste and requirement.

Our representative will call on you on 27th January in the afternoon. He is fully authorised to negotiate the terms and conditions of the business. He will also bring with him a few samples of our furniture for your inspection. Meanwhile, we are enclosing our catalogue and pricelists. These will help you in negotiating terms and conditions of business when our representative calls on you on 27th of this month.

Soon after the visit of our man we expect a good trial order so as to enable you to see for yourself the high uniform quality of material and finish of our furniture. We are sure our furniture would give to you and your customers lasting satisfaction and good value for the money spent.

Yours faithfully

Michael Tsong

3. *Letter from an Individual Customer Enquiring about Kitchen-installation*

37 Mountbatten Road
Singapore

12 June, 19...

The Manager
Electralux Homecare Centre
Tampines Road
Wind Tai Industrial Centre
Singapore

Dear Sir

I have been fascinated with kitchen systems installed in the kitchen of one of my very fast friends, and she has passed on your address to me.

I am interested in installation of complete kitchen system in my house. I have a new constructed flat and want to install some latest cooking devices etc. in my kitchen. I, therefore, would feel grateful if you send your latest illustrated catalogue and pricelist about it. Moreover, I would like that you send your consultant to help me plan the installation to suit my taste and place.

I am interested in kitchen equipment which is latest in design with practical innovation. I also want prompt delivery and installation after the order. You must also ensure prompt and efficient after sales service and best value for my money.

I look forward to your immediate response and action in this matter.

Yours faithfully

Rosa Lim

4. *Letter Requesting for Catalogue and Pricelist*

ZENITH INDUSTRIES PTE LTD
Kim Keat Lane, Singapore

Telephone : 02-250 5676
14 March, 19...

The Manager Sales
Universal Electric Company
12, Industrial Park
Jalan Kemajuan
Singapore

Dear Sir,

We manufacture and sell wide range of electrical equipment. We also sell electrical equipment of other reputed companies through our wholesale and retail outlets in Singapore. We are interested in your electrical equipments, specially explosion flame proof light-fittings and electrical equipment-for explosive atmosphere.

Therefore, will you please send us a copy of your catalogue and pricelist of the above items together with trade terms and conditions and descriptive literature which may be passed on to prospective buyers and customers.

We hope you shall quote the lowest price you are prepared to accept for our future repeat bulk orders for these items.

We look forward to your immediate response and action.

Yours faithfully

Ngkim Seng
Manager

5. *Reply to the above*

UNIVERSAL ELECTRIC COMPANY
12, Industrial Park, Jalan Kemajuan
Singapore

Telephone : 03-757 2928
Fax : 603-757 0501

The Manager
Zenith Industries Pte. Ltd.
Kim Keat Lane, Singapore

Dear Mr. Seng

Thank you for your interest in our electrical equipment, particularly in items most suited for explosive atmosphere. We are pleased to enclose the required information requested in the form of our illustrated catalogue, pricelist and related leaflets meant to be passed on to the customers.

We may tell you that we are sole agents of many electrical brand equipments including explosion-proof electrical fitting, enclosures, cable tiles and wiring products, fire and heat resistant cables, marine cables, screened cables, insulation terminal lugs etc. in Malaysia and Singapore. All our products are of high international standard and uniform quality. In case you have any further enquiry you are free to call. We can be reached between our working hours on all the working days.

However, our representative Mr. Joseph Gomez will call on you some time next week, but of course, after having fixed an appointment with you on telephone. Mr. Gomez is fully authorised to settle the terms and conditions of business on behalf of our company. We have instructed him to fix an appointment with you over telephone some time at your convenience in the next week.

We look forward to the opportunity of having long lasting and fruitful business relations with you.

Yours faithfully

James Lau

6. *Letter of Enquiry about Carpets etc.*

SUNFLAG FURNISHING SDN. BHD.
Jalan Jejka Dua, Taman Maluri
Cheras, Kuala Lumpur

20th March, 19...

Telephone : 03-958 5255
Fax : 03-958 0442

The Manager
Bintang Enterprises
Jalan Ipoh, Kuala Lumpur

Dear Sir,

We have been informed that you keep a large stock of imported high quality carpets and rugs for wholesale.

We are a large dealer in various furnishing items like carpets, rugs, curtains, wall-papers, blinds etc. We also provide carpet and rug shampooing. We buy these different items from various sources, but now feel interested in products stocked and sold by you in wholesale.

We can assure you of our repeat orders in bulk if your prices are competitive and the carpets are of high uniform quality and standard. We are particularly interested in your Persian and Kashmiri carpets to cater to the needs of our rich customers and clients.

Therefore, we shall feel obliged if you send us soon your latest catalogue and full details of payment and discount allowed on large and repeat purchase together with sample pieces you can let us have.

We look forward to your immediate reply and action in this matter.

Yours sincerely

Low Teng
Manager

7. Reply to the above

BINTANG ENTERPRISES
Jalan Epoh, Kuala Lumpur

Telephone : 03 621 8192
Fax : 03 621 5029

The Manager
Sunflag Furnishing Sdn. Bhd.
Jalan Jejka Dua, Taman Maluri
Cheras, Kuala Lumpur

Dear Mr. Teng,

We thank you for your keen interest in our carpets and your letter of 20th March and enclose our illustrated catalogue and pricelist giving detailed information as requested.

We are sending a full range of our primium carpets and rugs separately by a bearer and these consist of one square foot sample pieces of Persian and Kashmiri carpets to give you a fair idea of our excellent and highly prized genuine woollen carpets. However, we would request you to pay us a personal visit at our showroom to have a look and feel of our luxurious wide selection of carpets imported from India and Iran. We also have relatively cheaper varieties.

We allow 30% trade discount on repeat large orders of the value of not less than $ 50,000 each. Moreover, we allow an additional 7% discount of net price for payments within one month from receipt of our invoice.

We are sure you will find our trade terms and conditions attractive and our samples irresistible. We wish you become soon one of many proud and well satisfied bulk buyers of our quality carpets.

With thanks.

Yours faithfully

Alfred Wong
Manager (Sales)

LEE MARKETING SDN. BHD.
Sungei Wang Plaza, Kuala Lumpur

10 April, 19... Telephone : 07-548909
Fax : 07-545828

The Manager
Teow Hong Umbrella Pte Ltd.
Shenton Way, Mas Building
Singapore

Dear Sir

We have been informed that you manufacture various types of quality umbrellas and parasoles.

Of late we have received several enquires about umbrellas manufactured by you from our individual customers. And so we feel interested in your quality products.

Perhaps you might be aware that we are large dealers in all kinds of umbrellas: advertising umbrellas, promotional and corporate umbrellas, besides umbrellas used by individual man, woman and children. We also deal in garden and hawkerstall umbrellas.

There is a good market for quality cloth and PVG nylon umbrellas in our area and we can assure you of repeat bulk orders provided the prices are competitive and reasonable and the quality of uniform high standard. However, before placing a regular order, we shall be glad if you would send us a selection of 100 quality umbrellas for men, women and children on 20 days, approval. Any of these umbrellas unsold at the end of this period of 20 days would be returned to you at our own cost as we don't want to keep them as stock. We may mention here that this 'goods on approval' order is just for only this transaction. Later when we place repeat regular orders and shall keep the unsold items as stock.

We look forward to your early and favourable response.

Yours faithfully

Wang Ming Lee

9. Letter Requesting Quotation for Crockery

MODERN POTTERY PTE LTD
Orchard Road, Palais Renaissance
Singapore

11 April, 19... Telephone : 340 5199

The Manager
China Pottery (M) Sdn., Bhd.
Kuala Lumpur
Wisma Stephens

Dear Sir

We were glad to receive a supply of Bone China and Hotel China items of crockery last month from you. Now we would be glad if you would quote for the items named as under and manufactured by Sasaki Pottery Company of Japan. The items we need are listed in your latest catalogue of January 19... at number 5, 7, 9, 11, 15 and 16 respectively.

500 Teacups with saucers (Zen China)
300 Rice plates full size (Hotel China)
500 Mugs small sized (Bone China)
100 1/2 litre teapots (Viterous China)
300 Flowerpots (Zen China)
200 Sitting Buddha decoration pieces (Pearl China)

Price quoted should be inclusive of packing and delivery charges to the above address. Please also state the trade discount allowed, terms of payment and the date of earliest possible delivery.

Yours faithfully

Loh Tack Foo
Manager

10. Enquiry about Books on Sale or Return Basis

ACADEMIC BOOKS SUPPLY CO.
301, Orchard Road, Singapore

18 June, 19... Telephone : 2351563

The Manager
Asiapac Books Pte. Ltd.
Allunied Road
Singapore

Dear Sir

We have been engaged in the business of selling books, newspapers and periodicals for the last 8 years and are sole agents for the sale of a couple of reputed magazines and periodicals in the area.

In recent times we have received several enquiries about your books in Chinese and English about technical subjects and comics. We are interested in stocking and selling these books as well. Therefore, please send your latest catalogue of books and pricelist together with your trade terms soon.

Please let us also know if you can supply us your books on technical subjects and comics for children 'on sale or return' basis. We would like to have your books on credit and for that purpose we can provide you a couple of excellent bank and trade references. We shall clear your account every 2 months.

We hope to receive your early response.

Yours faithfully

Lee So Wah
Manager

11. *A Buyer's Letter Requesting Better Terms*

SUNSHINE ENTERPRISE
Central Market, Kuala Lumpur

15 March, 19... Telephone : 032823439

The Manager
Eminent Luggage Enterprise
Jalan Jejaka, Taman, Maluri
Cheras, Kuala Lumpur

Dear Sir

Thanks for your letter of 5 March, and for the samples of school-bags in polyester sent separately. I like these school bags, their quality, design and fast attractive colours. I hope these would become soon popular among school going students here if sincere and vigorous efforts are made coupled with right kind of advertisement of which I think I am quite capable of. But in my opinion your prices are too high even for these quality school bags in polyester.

I will have to make special efforts to introduce and popularise these bags among school-going students, and this means extra expenses on my part. Therefore, if I accept the quotation of your prices, that would leave me with no profit margin at all.

However, I may suggest you to allow me 40% trade discount instead of 30% on my purchases so that I may have a reasonable profit margin on my sales. That can certainly help me in placing a large order immediately. If you cannot allow me this increased trade discount then I must politely decline your present offer.

Yours faithfully

S.M. Yong

12. Reply to the above

EMINENT LUGGAGE ENTERPRISES
Jalan Jejka, Taman Maluri Cheras
Kuala Lumpur

Telephone : 03-985 8654
Fax : 03-983 2021

Mr. S.M. Yong
Sunshine Enterprise
Central Market
Kuala Lumpur

Dear Mr. Yong

Thanks for your letter of 15 March in response to our quotation for supply of school bags in polyester. But I am surprised to note that you have found our prices on the higher side, and so prohibitive. We manufacture these and other bags in large numbers and supply them to the whole of the area and beyond. As such we can maintain the prices of these bags as reasonable and low as possible without compromising the quality of these items. Consequently, they are very popular and in great demand. Sometimes we are in short supply of these inspite of our best efforts and over 100% capacity utilisation of our manufacturing facilities.

In view of the quality, design, durability etc. of these bags, I don't feel the prices quoted by me are too much. However, I don't want to disappoint you and am ready to allow you trade discount of 40% on all your purchases instead of usual 30%. But at the same time I must make it clear that it is the maximum I can do to help you as a special case.

I hope this should satisfy you to place an immediate order with us.

Yours faithfully

Soo Kok Kwong
Manager

THREE

ORDERS AND THEIR EXECUTION

Orders are the requests for despatch and delivery of goods or the rendering of services either against payment or on credit. Not unlike enquiries and their replies, the orders, their acknowledgement and execution fall under routine correspondence, yet they should not be treated casually. They deserve your full consideration and prompt attention. Orders and their replies should be as precise, clear, brief, direct and courteous as any other type of business letter. The writing of these is not as simple and a tame affair as is often thought.

Standard printed forms are being used for this purpose by many companies as these help to a great extent in avoiding errors with regard to the quantity, size and other specifications. When a printed order form is used, it should always have a covering letter. But small traders and businessmen may not have printed forms and so they may place order for goods by writing simple letters. Orders should be exact and clear with regard to the terms of payment trade discount, mode and schedule of delivery, specification of goods, quantity etc.

Orders should immediately be acknowledged with due courtesy. In your letter of acknowledgement also mention the details of the order and the date when it is going to be executed. In case the order is defective, you should tactfully seek the required information without offending the buyer. The processing of orders should be done very carefully. For this purpose printed forms may be used which facilitate in alloting job numbers, stock location, prices delivery schedule etc.

1. *Order for a Cordless Telephone and a Receive-Amplifier*

SINGAPORE TELEPHONE PTE LTD
20 Cecil Street, Singapore

10 July, 19... Telephone : 235 4416

The Manager Sales
Thomas Communication
Defu Lane, Singapore

Dear Sir

We hereby confirm the telephone order we placed with you yesterday evening in response to your quotation of 1st July for the following :

1. 14 'GENESIS' brand cordless telephones
   Price : S$ 200 each, less 40% trade discount

2. 10 'GENESIS' brand receive-amplifier
   Price : S$ 150 each, less 35% trade discount

The above items should be delivered to our above address within a week's time from the receipt of this order by your delivery van carriage paid. We are enclosing an account payee cheque for S$ 7000 towards part payment of these items and the balance of S$ 2075 would be paid on delivery. Send with the consignment the operating and maintaining instructions brochures which may be distributed among the customers and clients along with these devices. Also send the guarantee cards and cashmemo.

Kindly acknowledge the receipt of the cheque by return of post.

With thanks, we look forward to the delivery of the above within the scheduled time.

Yours faithfully

David Smith
Manager

Encl : As above

2. *Acknowledgement of the above*

12 July, 19... Telephone : 233 1516

Mr. Daniel Smith
Singapore Telephone Pte. Ltd.
20 Cecil Street
Singapore

Dear Mr. Smith

We thank you for your order of 10 July for 14 Genesis brand cordless phones and 10 receive-amplifier @ $ 200 and 150 each respectively with usual trade discount.

These items would be delivered by the week end without fail by our delivery van carriage paid along with guarantee cards, maintenance manual etc. We also acknowledge your cheque for S $ 7000 being its part payment of these telephone systems. The balance may be paid at the time of delivery by account payee cheque.

We are sure you will find these most satisfying as these are well-known for their trouble-free calls. We may again assure that these communication items are sophisticated ones designed with state-of-the-art clear reception, minus all the problems associated with ordinary phones. Receive-amplifiers are also of the same high international standard. Moreover, these are small, light and powerful and fit easily in pocket or purse. All you have to do is plug it on to a module phone. You can hear phone calls better wherever your are.

We thank you for this trial order and hope to receive repeat orders for large number of these and other similar instruments. We assure you of our fullest cooperation ever.

Yours faithfully

Jaffar Hussain

3. *Order for a Watch from an Individual Customer*

12 Sophia Road
Singapore

9 January, 19...

The Manager
Royal Watches Pte. Ltd.
Beach Road
Singapore

Dear Sir

I was really fascinated by Raymond Weil's brand watch 'Amadeus'. I saw it decorating the wrist of one of my friends. It is the latest product of the well-known Raymond Weil, a Swiss watch company and I want to have one such watch renown for its great precision and accuracy. My friend has given me your address.

I want it in deep blue colour with matching leather strap. I shall feel obliged if you can send it latest by 16th of January because I am likely to leave Singapore on 17th January on a business trip to Bangkok and Tokyo. You may send it by a courier at my own expense. I am enclosing a cheque for S$ 300.50 towards its cost and would pay the delivery charges at the time of delivery.

Please acknowledge the receipt of the order and cheque by return of post. Also intimate me the date of despatch. I look forward to your immediate response and action.

Yours faithfully

Jewel Lee

4. *Reply to the above*

ROYAL WATCHES PTE LTD
Beach Road, Singapore

12 January, 19...

Telephone : 220 4429
Fax : 220 4356

Mr. Jewel Lee
12 Sophia Road
Singapore

Dear Mr. Lee

We thank you for your order of 9 January for a watch 'Amadeus' brand of Raymond Weil of Switzerland. We are glad to receive you as one of the well satisfied and really discerning customers of ours. Soon you would be a proud possesser of this famous brand watch from Raymond Weil of Geneva. We also acknowledge the receipt of your cheque for S$ 300.50 towards its cost. You would be glad to know that you will receive the watch free of delivery charges and in a very beautiful gift pack specially created for this particular watch.

You may receive the watch perhaps before this letter reaches you. We shall send it day after tomorrow by our courier Mr. Novel Benjamin to your address given in the letter of order. In precision and accuracy it matches favourably with the beating of a healthy and vibrant heart of a person. In beauty and elegance it is the last word.

We once again thank you for your order and perfect choice.

Yours faithfully

Martin Teo

5. *Letter Placing an Order*

SUPER MARKETING PTE LTD
Eu Tong Sen Street, Singapore

8 February, 19... Telephone : 227 7503

The Manager
Peninsula Pte. Ltd.
Singapore

Dear Sir

Thank you for your quotation of 1st January, 19... and sample cakes of your deodorant premium toilet soap 'Swan Personal'. We are glad to place an order for 25 gross of 'Swan Personal' toilet soap cakes at the rates given in your catalogue excluding the forwarding and packing charges. We also agree to your trade discount of 25%, but we want that the consignment must reach us within 15 days of the placing of this order with you. For us the time factor and delivery schedule is of utmost importance and so we insist on the specified time schedule and reserve the right to refuse to take delivery of the consignment in case of its reaching us late.

Our cheque to cover your bill will be sent as soon as the goods reach us and are found satisfactory. Please take proper care in packaging the goods so that they may reach us in good condition.

Yours faithfully

Wong Shee Fun

6. *Letter Regetting Delay in Supply*

RAMZAN TRADERS
62, Shahrah-e-Quaid-e Azam
Lahore-54000 (Pakistan)

7, July 19...

Telephone : 253601
Fax : 9442-293789

Mr. Saeed Khan
Aman Trading Pvt. Ltd.
7/5, Zaibunnisa Street
Karachi-5 (Pakistan)

Dear Mr. Khan

Thank you for your order dated 30 June for 100 leather jackets and 250 pairs of leather gloves. We are pleased to note that you have been able to sell all the items in leather which you had ordered and received early last month. Truly, our leather goods are very popular as they are genuine, reasonably priced and durable. Consequently we are always in short supplies these days in spite of our over 110% capacity utilization in production in our two large factories.

Since these items are not in stock at present, we feel sorry that we are unable to despatch these immediately. We, therefore, expect to execute your order by 15th of August. By that time there would be an appreciable improvement in supply. We hope you will bear with us till then.

Yours faithfully

Niyamat Ali
Manager

7. *Follow-up Letter as the Order is Incomplete*

AKTHAR PLASTICS & CHEMICALS
69-C, P.E.C.H. Society, Off. Tariq Road
Karachi-75400 (Pakistan)

10 October, 19...

Telephone : 433666
433777
Fax : 221-433888

Mr. Shamshad Hussain
Musafar & Musafar
Peshawar Cantt. (Pakistan)

Dear Mr. Hussain

We thank you for your order no. 5490 of 20th September for 300 pieces of our moulded plastic chairs. We are ready to despatch the consignment and your order is in process. But you have not mentioned the type of chairs you want. As you are well aware that we have three types : CHR 1000, CHR 1001 and CHR 1003. They all are of the same price but CHR 1000 is with a cane look and CHR 1001 is purely for children and the last one, that is CHR 1003 is circular in design. These chairs with high backrest and superior leg designs are very popular and in great demand. These are manufactured using ultraviolet stablised polypropelene to withstand environmental stress and radiation. Therefore, we are sometimes in short supply. Since you are our old and trusted customer, we are filling your order on priority.

Kindly send immediately the details of the type of chairs you want to be sent. You may indicate your requirement on the margin or bottom of this letter and mail it back to us by return of post so that we may despatch your consignment at the earliest.

We are pleased to let you know that recently we have introduced a very attractive multi-purpose plastic table TBL-A1. It cost Rs. 390, can be converted to suit any house—a study table, a centre table or a casual sitout table. Moreover, it is available in a premium carry away gift pack. We are enclosing an illustrated catalogue about this attractive new offer of ours.

It is really a fore-runner of a whole new range of our new and whole fascinating products. We are sure you would like to order for these tables as well.

We look forward to your immediate reply.

Yours faithfully

Abdul Rehman
Manager

8. *Letter Notifying Partial Execution of an Order*

SAY TRADING PVT LTD
45, Bank Road, Rawalpindi

18 September, 19...

Telephone : 653287
Fax : 9251 654891

The Manager
The Moon & Star Agencies
22A/22, Gulberg II
Lahore-54660 (Pakistan)

Dear Sir

We thank you for your trial order of 10th September, 19... In accordance to your order, we have despatched today all the items except that at serial no. 7, code no. 15 as it is at present out of stock. We hope to send this item (Half-turn Foam-flow fittings), by the end of the next month as this would be readily available by then.

We have handed over the invoice, bill of landing and other relevant documents to Messers Akbar Ali & Sons, and have instructed them to forward these goods to you. These are insured against all risks, and the above mentioned forwarding agent is authorised to receive all their dues from you.

With these goods we have enclosed a sufficient number of our catalogues, pricelists and promotional material for distribution to customers and prospective buyers. We hope you will receive all these goods in perfect condition as they have been very carefully packed.

We look forward to your another bulk order in near future.

Yours faithfully

Mohmad Ibrahim

9. *Letter Notifying Delay in Execution of an Order*

WRITING INSTRUMENT PTE LTD
Brass Basah Complex, Singapore

4 March, 19...

Telephone : 338 7886
Fax : 336 1751

The Manager
Lee Fu Stationary Supplier
Genting Lane, Kheng Seng Building
Singapore

Dear Sir

We very much regret the delay in the execution of your order no. 754 of 20th February, 19... for our premium disposable Rotemaca brand ball-pens and refills. We knowledge your reminder and telephonic talk today in the morning.

However, we are really sorry to say that there has been some labour problem and strike by the workers in our factory during the second fortnight of the last month. Consequently, the production had come to a complete halt and no supplies could be despatched as all office-work and correspondence had been completely paralysed. That is why your earlier reminder remained unanswered.

Now the situation has considerably improved and production has started as a settlement has been made with the labour union to the satisfaction of both the parties. Hence, we shall spare no efforts to clear the accumulated orders on war footing during the ensuing days. We want to assure you that your consignment will be sent within 15-20 days.

You will be glad to know that we shall pay ourselves the delivery and transport charges to compensate you for this unforeseen delay and inconvenience.

We hope you shall bear with us for a little more time.

Yours faithfully

Wong Chew Ho
Manager Sales

10. *Letter Showing Inability to Execute an Order*

VICTORIA AGENCIES
22A/22, Gulberg II
Lahore-54660 (Pakistan)

10 March, 19...

Telephone : 877 917
Fax : 9242-877846

Mr. Salim Akhtar
12, Station Road
Multan (Pakistan)

Dear Mr. Akhtar

We thank you for your order of Ist March, 19... requesting us to supply you three sets of our technology-intensive electronic kitchen machine 'Top Spin' with a unique inter-locking system. We also acknowledge the receipt of your demand draft to us the full and final payment towards the purchase of these food mixers. However, we regret our inability to supply these at present because we already have many urgent orders from our distributors and wholesale agents besides some export orders. And we are committed to supply our food-mixers to them on priority basis.

We may frankly confess that in spite of our best efforts and more than 150% capacity utilization of our production facilities, we have not been able to cope with the rush of orders from our agents, distributors, individual customers like you and foreign buyers.

The demand is so great of these kitchen machines that we are meeting the orders strictly 'first come first served' basis and no party or individual is being favoured at the cost of others.

We can keep you on our waiting list and assure you of the deiivery just after one month from now on the condition that you confirm your order by return of post with the time stipulation attached.

We look forward to your immediate reply.

Yours faithfully

Suleman Seth
General Manager

11. *Letter Notifying Cancellation of an Order*

16 March, 19...

12, Station Road
Multan (Pakistan)

Mr. Suleman Seth
Victoria Agencies
22A/22, Gulberg II
Lahore (Pakistan)

Dear Mr. Seth

This is with reference to my order dated 1st March, 19... for three sets of kitchen machines 'Topspin' and your reply dated 10 March showing your inability to supply them immediately.

These food mixures were urgently needed as they were to be given as gifts in the marriage of my sisters. Since, now I have arranged to get these from another source, however of another brand and from another company, I no more need your food-mixers and therefore request you to cancel the above order.

The demand draft sent towards the full and final payment of these three kitchen machines may be returned immediately as I urgently need this money for the purpose of marriage of my sisters.

I very much regret the inconvenience caused to you.

Yours faithfully

Salim Akhtar

12. *Reply to the above*

VICTORIA AGENCIES
22A/22, Gulberg II
Lahore - 54660 (Pakistan)

20 March, 19...

Telephone : 877917
Fax : 9242-8778

Dear Mr. Salim Akhtar

This has the reference to your recent letter of 16 March, 19... requesting the cancellation of your order of 1st March 19..., three sets of our food-mixers 'Topspin'.

We are really sorry that we could not supply these immediately which you needed to be given as gifts in the marriage of your dear sisters. As desired by you, we have cancelled your order and are returning your demand draft. Kindly acknowledge the receipt of it. However, convey our hearty congratulations to your sisters on the occasion of their marriages.

With best wishes.

Yours faithfully

Suleman Seth
General Manager

Encl : as Above

13. Letter from a Buyer Regretting Delay in Executing an Order

HIMALAYAN TRADING CENTRE
Red Cross Building, Bagh Bazar
Kathmandu (Nepal)

3 April, 19...

Teleophone : 224192

Mr. Roop Singh
Sunrise Enterprises & Suppliers
Bhotahity, Kathmandu
Nepal

Dear Mr. Singh

We thank you for you letter of 27th March, 19... but regret to say that you are not in a position to meet our demand of 600 pieces of hand-knitted woollen sweaters and pullovers in one consignment.

However, your consignment of 300 sweaters and pullovers has reached us and we are pleased to get it in time. We are really satisfied at the designs, quality of the woolthreads used and the knitting, but we feel that the packing has left much to be desired. Therefore, we want to underline the need for you to give special attention to this point. We hope that the next instalment of our consignment of 300 sweaters would reach us by the end of this month.

Yours faithfully

Shyam Bahadur
Manager

14. *Letter Acknowledging the Receipt of Goods*

SHAMSHEED AHMED & SONS
493, Rahimpura, Faislabad
(Pakistan)

6 February, 19... Telephone : 273815
273817

Mr. Ziaul Rehman
Ruksana Industries
44, Shahra-e-Quid-e-Azam
Hyderabad (Pakistan)

Dear Mr. Rehman

We are pleased to inform you that your consignment of 1200 packets of one kilogram each refined iodised salt 'Table top' has reached us today. The consignment has been received in a prefectly satisfactory condition. We are also in receipt of your bill of landing and other documents. We thank you for the prompt execution of our order and hope that in future also the same promptness would be shown in filling our orders.

Of late there have been continuous trade enquiries about your brand of salt packets which show that the item is becoming popular and is in large demand. Therefore, we are sure of selling the entire stock within a short period, and so you may expect our next order and for larger quantity very soon.

Yours faithfully

Inayat Hussain Rana

15. *Letter Notifying the Execution on Order*

SADEK INDUSTRIES PVT. LTD.
49, Azimpura, Dhaka-1205
(Bangladesh)

3 February, 19... Telephone : 507870

Mr. Nurual Hassan
Rehman & Co.
Sadar Bazar
Barisal (Bangladesh)

Dear Mr. Hassan

We are pleased to inform you that we have executed your order no. 472 of 25th January, 19... for electrical insulating, surface protection and surgical tapes. The consignment consists of three cases specially prepared and packed in waterproof-lined material. We have forwarded the relevant documents through your bankers.

A copy of our bill no. 3745, dated 1st February, 19... for Takas 5700 is enclosed for your prior information. Please release the documents immediately on presentation.

We are confident you will find the consignment to your entire satisfaction. We thank you for your trial order and look forward to repeat orders from you.

Yours faithfully

Chand Khan

16. *Letter Requesting for Forwarding Instructions*

PELENDUX TEXTILES
22, Jalan, 18/16A, 463 Petlang Jaya
Salangcr, Darul Eshan, Malaysia

4 January, 19...

Telephone : 7762222
Fax : 03-7762821

The Manager
Chou Chou & Co.
14, Kallang Avenue
Kallang Bahru Complex
Singapore-1233

Dear Sir

We are pleased to notify that the consignment of cotton and blanded fabrics ordered by you on 25 January, 19... is ready for despatch.

We have processed and filled your order on urgent basis by making some special efforts. You would appreciate that we have done it strictly according to our agreed time schedule in spite of our very busy schedule and rush of orders.

Now we await your immediate shipping instructions. As soon as we receive them we shall send you our advice of despatch and other related documents.

Yours faithfully

Abdul Rehman

FOUR

COMPLAINTS AND ADJUSTMENTS

In spite of our best intentions and efforts, there are occasions for making or dealing with a compliant. Complaints are inevitable in business because there are many factors over which you have no control. There might be complaints because the wrong consignment has been sent, poor service has been rendered, the quality of goods sent is not satisfactory, goods have been received in a damaged condition, the prices charged are high or the discount has been less than agreed etc. When there is a cause, a complaint should immediately and firmly be lodged in polite language. It is the fundamental right of a buyer to notify the supplier the problem and nature of the complaint and demand its prompt redressal.

Compliant should always be suggestive and result-oriented. You should clearly suggest a fair compensation and adjustment. Never hesitate to demand proper redressal and compensation on genuine grounds. Be brief, exact and clear in your complaint but avoid impoliteness. Complaints should be promptly answered to restore the buyer's goodwill and confidence. They should never be resented as they offer you an opportunity for self-analysis, improvement in quality or service. Your replies to complaints should always be tactful, prompt, polite and apologetic. State the reasons that led to the cause of complaint and the steps you intend to take for its timely redressal.

Never hesitate to own your fault frankly in respect of a genuine complaint. Always try to settle a complaint at the earliest, remembering that the customers is always right and that he is a king. In case the complaint is false, reject it firmly but politely. They should always be handled in such a way as to avoid long correspondence.

1. Complaint about Defective Goods

ABC TRADING CO.
641, Jalan Sentul Kuala Lumpur

5 April, 19... Telephone : 03-4412272

The Manger
Eagle Enterprise
Wisma Central, Kuala Lumpur

Dear Sir

We are sorry to say that recently we have received many complaints from our customers about your ball-pens and refills. They have not been giving desired satisfactory service in spite of the fact that they are relatively expensive and our customers buy them as items of value.

These items about which we have received complaints in person, in writing and also over phone, relate to the batch supplied against our order no. 540 of 20th March, 19... . This order was placed on the basis a few sample ball-pens and refills left with us by your representative. We have ourselves compared the samples with those supplied later and have noted that the latter are not upto the mark.

There is something wrong with these ball-pens and refills, particularly with their tips and ink. They leak, over flow and spoil the hands and apparels of the owners. Some of them blot off the sheet when writing. This is really unfortunate and regrettable.

Therefore, we want you to immediately replace the consignment and take away the pens and refills still left with us out of this lot. Please ensure that this replacement lot should be without any defective ball pen and refill. These must be of expected quality and standard worth more for the value of the money spent by our customers.

Yours faithfully

Victor Lim

2. *Complaint about Unsatisfactory Service of a Washing Machine*

12 July, 19...

17 Cheleng Hon Street
Bangkok

Mr. Suchinda Chonavan
Sian Stores Limited Partnership
204, Sian Square
Bangkok (Thailand)

Dear Mr. Chonavan

I am sorry to report that a semi-automatic twin tub 'Wash Well' washing machine bought from you a month ago vide receipt no. 4475 dated 11 June, 19... has started giving some trouble. Its motor starts making some subdued whirring sound if loaded to its full capacity of 4 kg. Its spin-dry system also does not make the clothes considerably dry. Moreover, its inlet hose connection switch does not function smoothly and it requires much pressure to make it operate. The spinner lid has also developed a hairy crack. It is with a 2 year warranty. The energy consumptions is on higher side as well.

I take a very poor view of the situation as it is an expensive item and you have made very tall claims in your advertisements and brochures about the efficiency and efficacy of your washing machines.

I, therefore, request you to advise me immediately as what should I do in the matter. Would you send your mechanic to remove these defects? I would prefer to have a trouble-free replacement piece at the earliest. However, I look forward to your immediate response and action in the matter.

Yours faithfully

Narapath Suphlong

3. *Reply to the above Complaint*

31 AM STORES LTD PARTNER SHIP
204, Sian Square, Bangkok

16 July, 19...

Telephone : 251 6284
Fax : 251 3812

Dear Mr. Suphlong

We are in receipt of you letter dated 12 July, 19... and regret that your washing machine is not giving satisfactory service. However, the complaint made by you has surprised us all here because all our models are equipped with heavy duty motors to give continuous trouble free long service at a stretch. Similarly, the spin-dry system is equally of high international standard to leave the clothes considerably dry.

The claims made in our advertisements are not tall claims, they are a reality. Our machines are hardworking to give the best value of your money. It is for the first time that we have received such a compliant.

Our mechanic would pay you a visit soon to find out what is wrong with the washing machine and how it has developed these defects.

We are sorry for the inconvenience.

Yours faithfully

Suchinda Chanavan
Manager Sales

4. *Complaint about Non-delivery of Goods*

SONGSWANG BROTHERS LTD
24, Bangkok Road, Chugmai
(Thailand)

9 April, 19...

Telephone : 637821
Fax : 642683

Mr. Chattchan Thanarat
Orapin & Uravin
2, Phya Thai Road
Bangkok-10330
(Thailand)

Dear Mr. Thanarat

On 25th March, 19... we placed an order over phone and then sent a written order confirming it for 5 gross umbrellas and similar number of raincoats. We had underlined that the goods must reach us within 10 days, but we regret to say that the consignment has not been received here till now. Your failure to appreciate the urgency of our order has put us in a very embarrassing situation as we are not in a position to satisfy our customers and keep our promise made to them. It also means a loss of business besides loss of a face.

I, therefore, urge you to despatch the ordered items immediately, or treat our order as cancelled. We shall obtain these from some other reliable source.

Yours faithfully

Suchinda Pramaj

5. *Reply to the above*

ORAPIN & URAVIN
2, Phya Thai Road, Bangkok

12 April, 19...

Teleophone : 2512200
2512223
Fax : 2183921

Mr. Suchinda Pramaj
Song Swang Brothers Ltd.
24, Bangkok road, Chungmai

Dear Mr. Pramaj

We are in receipt of you letter of complaint dated 9th April, 19... and regret to note that the items ordered have not reached you so far. We apologize for this delay and hope that this has not caused much inconvenience to you.

The reason for this delay is that the person who processes the orders suddenly developed a heart problem and was sent for hospitalisation. His substitute is a new one who under the pressure of rush of orders, has misplaced your order unintentionally.

Your order has now been processed and the consignment is almost ready for despatch and it would reach you within 3 days. To compensate the inconvenience caused by us to you by our delayed supply, we shall pay for the transport and delivery charges.

However, we want to assure you that such a mistake will not be committed in future and goods would be sent strictly according to the time schedule as in the past.

We once again apologize for the delay and inconvenience.

Yours faithfully

Chattichan Thanarat

6. *Complaint about Goods Received in Excess*

JOLLY HARDWARE (M) SDN BHD
Jalan San Peng, Kuala Lampur

10 December, 19... Telephone : 03-222 8066

Mr. Wee Chong Lai
Eagle Hardware Sdn. Bhd.
200, Jalan Station
Ipoh

Dear Mr. Lai

We are pleased to have received our consignment in time and thank you for prompt execution of our order. However, on opening the consignment, we found that it contained 120 dozen paint brushes and 150 dozen security padlocks, far in excess to our order.

We had ordered only for 20 dozen of paint brushes and 50 dozen security padlocks and you have charged us for these number of items. The rest of the hardware items have been received as per our order.

Perhaps the mistake must have occurred while collecting the various items for our consignment. In a normal course we would ask you to send us a new bill for the items in excess, but our present requirement of these two items is so fully met that we are sorry not to ask for a new bill. We don't feel it prudent to block the money and space for this surplus stock.

Pending your instruction as to how these items should be returned to you, we are holding these items supplied in excess.

Yours sincerely

Peter Chew
Manager

7. *Complaint Regarding Receipt of Wrong Goods*

ROYAL ENTERPRISES PVT LTD
129, Stadium Road, Dhaka
(Bangladesh)

4 June, 19... Telephone : 247381

Mr. Ismail Khan
Ishan Leatherites
92 Hanif Market
Chittagong (Bangladesh)

Dear Mr. Khan

Thank you for your prompt execution of our order of 25th April, 19... . We took the delivery of the consignment today in the morning. The consignment was in perfect order, but to our great surprise we found altogether different shoe-uppers, however, the soles, belts and jackets were what we had actually ordered.

We had placed order for 500 pairs of shoe-uppers for men's shoes and not for ladies' shoes. If you refer again you will find that the shoe-uppers sent by you don't correspond with our order no. 3321 dated 25th April. The shoe-uppers for ladies' shoes are not required at all by us because there is already a sufficient stock of it with us.

Evidently wrong items have been sent to us and it has caused as a great inconvenience as we have many urgent order for men's shoes only. Please let us know immediately by return of post when we will receive the correct shoe-uppers. Meanwhile we are holding the goods with us which we have not ordered.

We look forward to hear soon from you.

Yours faithfully

Hanif Ansari

8. *Reply to the above*

ISHAN LEATHERITES
92, Hanif Market, Chillangong
(Bangladesh)

8 June, 19... Telephone : 783215

Mr. Hanif Ansari
Royal Enterprises Pvt. Ltd.
129, Stadium Road, Dhaka
(Bangladesh)

Dear Mr. Ansari

We are in receipt of your complaint of 4 June, 19... and really feel sorry to learn that you have received one of the items wrong. We regret and apologize for the inconvenience caused to you. In fact, the mistake was on the part of our order processor-cum-despatch personnel.

This mistake should not have occurred at all as all the consignments are usually checked and carefully packed before despatch. We want to assure you that such mistake would never take place in future. However, we have seriously dealt with the matter to fix responsibility.

We are despatching today the 500 pairs of shoe-uppers of men's shoes as ordered by you and these are likely to reach you within 2-3 days. Once again we regret the mistake and apologize for the inconvenience caused by us.

Yours faithfully

Ismail Khan
Manager

9. *Complaint about Wrong Statement*

THOMAS & THOMAS
Shahrah-e-Liquate Opp. Odean Cinema
Karachi (Pakistan)

2 January, 19...

Telephone : 5681111
5681113

Mr. Iqbal Qureshi
49 Rahimpura
Faislabad (Pakistan)

Dear Mr. Qureshi

We have just received our statement for the month of December, 19... on our charge account no. 277. The statement shows a purchase of 250 T-Shirts for Rs. 3,750. We are cocksure that we did not place any such order.

The purchase was supposedly made on 3rd December, but infact I was not here in the city on that date. I had been on business trip for a few days to Iran and no one else was authorised to make use of this account. Therefore, we are sure there is some mistake somewhere. However, all the other items in this statement are correct and tally with our records.

I am enclosing a cheque for Rs. 72,500 for the balance amount after deducting Rs. 3,750. I shall feel favoured if you look immediately into the matter so that my account may be cleared.

Yours sincerely,

Faiz Ahmed
Manager

10. *Reply to the above Complaint*

NAEEM AHMED & SONS
49 Rahimpura, Faislabad (Pakistan)

10 January, 19... Telephone : 273815
237817

The Manager
Thomas & Thomas
Shahrah-e-Liaquat
Opp. Odean Cinema
Karachi (Pakistan)

Dear Mr. Ahmed

We are in receipt of your complaint regarding despatch of a wrong statement for the month of December, 19... We regret to state that you were billed for a purchase of 150 T-shirts @ Rs. 150 each which you had really not ordered for. We acknowledge the error in the statement and express our deep apologies.

As such the sum of Rs. 3,750 has been deleted from your account. We also acknowledge the receipt of your cheque for Rs. 72,500 towards the settlement of your account.

We thank you once again for bringing to our notice the above mistake, and we assure you we will check such errors in the future. We look forward to your early next order and assure you of our best cooperation ever.

Yours sincerely

Iqbal Qureshi
Manager

11. *Letter in Response to a Complaint about a Defective Carpet*

APEX CARPETS & FURNISHINGS
15, Thonburi, Avenue, Bangkok (Thailand)

12 March, 19...

Telephone : 639829

Dear Mr. Suchindra Sakhon

We thank you for your letter of 5th March, 19... but feel really sorry to note your complaint about the carpet you purchased from us last month. The complaint that the carpet supplied by us has a big spot and its strands are coming out at one place has surprised us. Our items are premium ones manufactured with utmost care and skill by expert craftsmen and so we are rather confounded by your compliant. Therefore, we have instructed our representative to call on your residence to make an on the spot study of the defect in the carpet. He will call on you on 16th March, in the afternoon to inspect the carpet.

We may assure you that customers' satisfaction is our motto and want to help you in the matter. If your complaint is genuine and our representative confirms it, we shall be much pleased to send immediately a replacement carpet. Please be assured of our fullest cooperation in the matter to your entire satisfaction without any delay. We once again regret the inconvenience caused to you.

Yours faithfully

Pramoj Thanom

12. *Complaints about Goods Received in Damaged Condition*

SOUTHEAST COMPUTER SYSTEM SDN BHD
Damansara Uttama, Petaling Jaya, Malaysia

3 July, 19...

Telepohone : 03-7185390
03-7189011

The Manager Sales
Digital World Sdn. Bhd.
Wisma Damansara
Kuala Lumpur

Dear Sir

We are in receipt of the consignment containing 300 Maxell Floppy Disks sent by you against our order of 18 June, 19... The consignment was delivered yesterday late in the evening, when we were about to close the business for the day. Consequently, we received the consignment without properly examining to see whether it was in perfect order or not as it was closing time.

However, we regret to say that we found about a score of floppies damaged when we opened the consignment in the morning today. Perhaps these got damaged because of improper and careless handling at some stage before the packing.

I expect that these damaged disks would be soon replaced. We have kept them separately so that these may be inspected by your representative when he visits here. These may be collected in case you need them to support your claim from your suppliers.

We would humbly advise you that more care and improvement in the matter of handling the goods in future be taken so as to avoid damage and loss to you and inconvenience to your customers as well.

We look forward to your early response and action in the matter.

Yours faithfully

Abdul Sattar

13. Buyer's Complaint about Delivery Charges

RATNA PONGSATHORN & CO
24, Phuntep Road, Phuket
(Thailand)

Telephone : 583621
Fax : 573826

The Sales Manager
Rama General Stores
212, Wang Burashaper
Bangkok (Thailand)

Dear Mr. Koman

When we placed our trial order with your representative when we called on us last time, we were given an undertaking that we would be provided free delivery. But to our surprise and annoyance we were charged with the cost of delivery.

This is something new, strange and in total violation of business morality and so we were constrained not to send our further orders. First we thought to keep silent over the matter but now we think that you should be informed about it. If you had been in our place, you too would have taken this matter as un-generous and unethical.

We look forward to your views and comments at the earliest.

Yours faithfully

Narapath Tharat

FIVE

STATUS AND TRADE REFERENCES

Credit facilities is the pivot on which all major business activities revolve. We cannot think of trade and business without these facilities which means 'buy now and pay later.' Business on large scale is almost impossible without a credit facilities. It helps buying goods and services without spot or immediate payment. It is a double blessing. It helps the buyer in increasing his working capital manifold. In return the supplier has more business and correspondingly more profits.

Credit facilities help in avoiding the botheration of payment each and every time a purchase is made. But there are some inherent risks in the system. For example, there is a risk of bad debts. Again there is a lot of extra work of keeping records and collecting outstanding. Moreover, the buyer has to pay a little extra on his purchases as he is taking goods on credit and on such terms as are more favourable to the supplier.

However, these risks can be eliminated or minimised by determining the credit worthiness and financial soundness of the other party before granting credit facilities. The supplier must know, well in advance, the buyer's capacity and willingness to pay for the goods supplied on credit. This can be done only through status and credit references and enquiries to banks, financial institutions, professional credit rating agencies and other companies having business dealings with the buyer. The professional credit rating agencies and bureaus keep the record and history of various companies in regard to their financial standings, and credit worthiness.

Letters seeking credit and status information should always be polite, confidential, formal and brief. A self-addressed and stamped envelope should always be enclosed with such a request for the convenience of the recipient. Letters in response to status and credit references should invariably be frank, factual brief and tactful. Letters refusing credits should be drafted more tactfully so as not annoy and offend the other party in any manner. Similarly, unfavourable or not so favourable opinions regarding credit worthiness should be expressed tactfully and cautiously.

1: *The Buyer's Request to Supply Goods on Credit*

BERITA DISTRIBUTORS
Jalan Tun Abdul Razak, Kuala Lumpur

9 September, 19...

Telephone : 03-2923123
Fax : 03-2825200

Mr. Sin Wah Hin
Patrick Bros. Sdn. Bhd.
Komplex Selangor
Jalan Sultan
50000 Kuala Lumpur

Dear Mr. Hin

Our business dealings with you have been almost one and half years old now. So far we have been supplied goods on cash basis but making payments each time on invoice has been quite inconvenient for us. Therefore, we would like to place this order and subsequent orders with you on open account with quarterly settlements. Our present order no. 735 for goods worth $ 15000 is enclosed.

If you need we can provide you with a number of excellent trade and bank references. Since we urgently need the goods ordered, we would feel obliged if the matter is expedited.

We hope to receive your early favourable response.

Yours faithfully

Teo Lek Kuan
Manager

2. *Supplier's Favourably Reply (I)*

PATRICK BROS SDN BHD
Komplex Selangor, Jalan Sultan
Kuala Lumpur

15 September, 19...

Telephone : 03-2312778
Fax : 03-2324486

Mr. Teo Lek Kuan
Berita Distributors
Jalan Tun Abdul Razak
Kuala Lumpur

Dear Mr. Kuan

We thank you for your recent order of 9th September for goods on credit worth $ 15000. Our business relations with you have become quite mature all these days and we have been fully satisfied in having repeated and extensive dealings during this period of one and half years. We ourselves were thinking to extend credit facilities to you on our own, but now here is your request.

We are pleased to inform you that your request for supply to goods on open account has been accepted. Now your transactions have been transferred from payment on invoice to open account with quarterly settlement. We are fully satisfied with regard to your sound financial status and credit worthiness and you need not supply us any such references.

Yours order no. 735 is being processed and the consignment would be despatched soon.

We look forward to our long lasting cordial and voluminous business relations for our mutual benefit based on quarterly settlement period.

Yours sincerely

Sin Wah Hin
Manager

3. *Supplier's Unfavourable Reply*

PATRICK BROS SDN BHD
Komplex Selangor, Jalan Sultan
Kuala Lumpur

15 September, 19...

Telephone : 03-2312778
Fax : 03-2324486

Mr. Teo Lek Kuan
Berita Distributors
Jalan Tun Abdul Razak
Kuala Lumpur.

Dear Mr. Kuan

Thank you for your order of 9th September for goods worth $ 15000 on credit with quarterly settlements. No doubt our transaction with you have been one and half years old, but we are sorry to say that we are not in a position to grant you open account facilities, at least for the present.

As far we understand your financial obligations have been too heavy to allow you a credit facility. In future, when your obligations are substantially reduced, you may again apply for an open account. Then your request would certainly be considered favourably.

We are really sorry that we are unable to grant you your request for open account transactions for the present although we would very much like to help you in the matter.

Yours faithfully

Sin Wah Hin
Manager

4. *The Supplier Asking for References*

PATRICK BROS SDN BHD
Komplex Selangor, Jalan Sultan
Kuala Lumpur

Telephone : 2312778
Fax : 03-2324 486

15 September, 19...

Mr. Teo Lek Kuan
Berita Distributors
Jalan Tun Abdul Razak
Kuala Lumpur

Dear Mr. Kuan

We thank you for your order of 9th September for goods worth \$ 15000 on credit with quarterly settlements. In this regard we would like you to send us three trade and bank references with whom you have had dealings. No doubt our business transactions have been one and half years old and they have become healthier and stronger during this period and we have been fully satisfied with you, but it is our practice to ask for there references whenever we are requested to supply goods on credit. We hope you will not mind it.

We look forward to receive this information soon. Meanwhile we have put your order in process so that it may be filled as soon as we hear from you.

Yours faithfully

Sin Wah Hin

BERDITA DISTRIBUTORS
Jalan Tun Abdul Razak
Kuala Lumpur

20 September, 19...

Telephone : 03-2923123
Fax : 03-2825200

Mr. Sin Wah Hin
Patrick Bros. Sdn. Bhd.
Komplex Selangor
Jalan Sultan
Kuala Lumpur

Dear Mr. Him

We thank you for your letter of 15th September, 19... asking in three trade and bank references. You may take up trade references with the following with which we have had extensive business and cash transactions for the last 7 years :

1. Goodtimes Marketing Pte. Ltd., Commonwealth Lane, Singapore, Telephone : 777 4922.

2. Eagle Hardware (M) Sdn. Bhd., Jalan San Peng, Kuala Lumpur, Telephone : 03-222 8066

3. United Malayan Banking Corpn. Bhd. Banking Hall, Jalan Sulaiman, Kuala Lumpur.

We hope you would immediately take up the references and send the goods ordered soon following the satisfactory responses from them. We may remind you that the goods are needed on urgent basis for early delivery to our clients and customers.

Yours faithfully

Teo Lek Kuan
Manager

6. *The Supplier takes up Reference with a Trader*

PATRICK BROS SDN BHD
Komplex Selangor, Jalan Sultan
Kuala Lumpur

24 September, 19...

Telephone : 03-2312778
Fax : 03-2324486

Mr. Victor James
Eagle Hardware (M) Sdn. Bhd
Jalan San Peng
Kuala Lumpur

Dear Mr. James

Berdita Distributors, Jalan Tun Abdul Razak, Kuala Lumpur telephone: 2923132, has placed on order with us for goods worth $ 15000 on credit and has given your name as a reference.

We shall be obliged if you let us have information regarding Berita Distributor's financial status and credit worthiness. We would like to know, in particular, how long Mr. Kuan have had been dealing with you and how far these dealings have been satisfactory and fruitful.

The information and facts supplied to us in this respect shall be treated strictly confidential. We enclose a stamped and self-addressed envelop for your convenience. We shall be glad to reciprocate to give you credit information when requested.

We look forward to your early response.

Yours faithfully

Sin Wah Hin
Manager

7. *Trader's Favourable Response*

EAGLE HARDWARE (M) SDN BHD
Jalan San Peng, Kuala Lumpur

Telephone : 222 8066

30 September, 19...

Mr. Sin Wah Hin
Patrick Bros. Sdn. Bhd.
Komplex Selangor
Jalan Sultan, Kuala Lumpur

Dear Mr. Hin

In response to your letter dated 24 September, 19... seeking information about the financial standing and credit worthiness of Berita Distributors, Jalan Tun Abdul Razak, Kuala Lumpur, we are happy to send you a favourable reply. This company has been in our business relation for the last 7 years and during these years we have never hesitated to trust them with goods worth any value of credit and there was not a single occasion when they defaulted in timely payment.

On the basis of our 7 years long experience with them we believe them to be highly credit worthy and financially sound.

The information given here may be treated as strictly confidential and is given without any responsibility on our part.

Yours faithfully

Munis Ooi
Manager

8. *Trader's Qualified Response*

Dear Mr. Hin

We thank you for your letter of 24 September, 19... requesting status and credit information about Berita Distributors, Jalan Tun Abdul Razak, Kuala Lumpur.

We inform you, in strict confidence, that we have been having business dealings with them for the last 7 years. These dealings have been very fruitful, but of late, things have not been as smooth as they were in the past. Since they have incurred some losses recently, they are finding it increasingly difficult to pay their dues in time and meet promptly their obligations.

They are trustworthy but in view of their recent decline in fortunes, you may supply them goods on credit in small quantity only. We are not sure how long it will take them to improve their bottom line. It may be in immediate future or it may take some more time.

Yours faithfully

Munis Ooi
Manager

9. *Trader's Unfavourable Response*

Dear Mr. Hin

Thank you for your letter of 24th September, 19... requesting credit and status information about the company referred to in your letter.

We inform you that the company you have referred is a close family concern of 3 brothers and their 2 nephews, and is operating on not a very large scale. Of late we have stopped supply of goods on credit to this party because our experience with them has not been encouraging in this regard. We had some difficulty is recovering our dues in time. It is also said that there is some dispute among the partners and soon there may be a division and split.

In the light of above facts and our own experience in recent days with the company, we would advise you to be cautious. The information may be treated as secret and strictly confidential.

Yours faithfully

Munis Ooi
Manager

10. *Bank's Favourable Reply*

UNITED MALAYAN BANKING CORPN BHD
Banking Hall, Jalan Sulaiman
Kuala Lumpur

1 October, 19... Telephone : 03-274 6044

Mr. Sin Wah Hin
Patrick Bros. Sdn. Bhd.
Komplex Selangor, Jalan Sultan
Kuala Lumpur

Dear Mr. Hin

We are glad to send you, in strict confidence, the status information about the company referred to in your letter of 24 September, 19...

Berita Distributors of Jalan Tun Abdul Razak, Kuala Lumpur has had current and savings accounts with us for the last 6 years. These accounts have always been in order with sufficient balance to cover all their withdrawls.

This company has borrowed from this bank more than 4 times during the last 6 years ranging from $ 10,000 to $ 25,000 and have never been a defaulter in repaying these loans and interest well in time. We are unaware of any outstanding debts they may have.

In our opinion this is a considerably reputed company and its credit worthiness is beyond any shadow of doubt.

This information is given in strict confidence and without any responsibility on our part.

Yours faithfully

Peter Corda
Manager

11. *Bank's Unfavourable Reply*

Dear Mr. Him

We are in receipt of your letter of 24 September, 19... seeking status enquiry about Berita Distributors, Jalan Tun Abdul Razak, Kuala Lumpur.

However, as far this firm's financial standing and credit worthiness is concerned, we don't have a favourable opinion. And as such, we would advise you not to extend a credit facility for such a large amount.

As their financial standing is doubtful, most of their suppliers deliver them goods on cash-on-invoice basis. Therefore, we would advise you caution to supply them goods on open account terms.

This information may be treated as secret and strictly confidential, and is given without any responsibility on our part.

Yours faithfully

Peter Corda
Manager

12. *Agency's Favourable Reply*

CREDIT SYNDICATE (M) SDN BHD
Jalan Jambur, Air Mawar, Kuala Lumpur

Telephone : 03-627 3544
Fax : 03-666 3512

28 September, 19...

Mr. Sin Wah Hin
Patrick Bros. Sdn. Bhd.
Komplex Selangor
Kuala Lumpur

Dear Mr. Hin

Thanks for your letter of 20 September, 19... requesting status and credit information about Berita Distributors, Jalan Tun Abdul Razak, Kuala Lumpur. We have required details about this company and have made further enquiries about it in the last 2-3 days. On the basis of these we are inclined to respond favourably.

We, therefore, don't hesitate to recommend Berita Distributors with regards to its sound financial standing and credit worthiness. You can trust them with goods worth any amount on credit they order from you time to time.

Berita Distributors has had business dealings with many other reputed large companies and suppliers and has open account with them. And there has been no adverse report or comments in recovering dues from them in time. However, the information is given in strict confidence.

Yours faithfully

M. Fergueson

13. *Agency's Unfavourable Reply*

Dear Mr. Hin

In response to your letter of 20 September, 19... seeking credit and status information about Berita Distributors, Jalan Tun Abdul Razak, Kuala Lumpur, we have updated and completed our enquiry and regret to report unfavourably.

Our enquiry reveals that a court-case is pending against this company for non-recovery of long overdue payments to a big supplier. The payment involved is quite large. The company is not well managed and therefore, it is running in losses. Of late most of the supplier's have stopped to have any business dealings with them or they make deliveries on cash payments only.

We, therefore, advise you to exercise caution and discretion in granting them their request of supplies on charge/open account.

Yours faithfully

M. Fergueson

14. *Supplier's Favourable Response - (II)*

PATRICK BROS SDN BHD
Komplex Selangor, Jalan Sultan
Kuala Lumpur

Telephone : 2312778
Fax : 03-2324 486

1 October, 19...

Mr. Teo Lek Kuan
Berita Distributors
jalan Tun Abdul Razak
Kuala Lumpur

Dear Mr. Kuan

We are fully satisfied with trade and bank references supplied by you vide your letter of 20 September, 19... Consequently your request for supply of goods on open account terms with quarterly settlement has been accepted.

Your order no. 735 for goods worth $ 15000 dated 9 September is now ready for despatch and will be delivered within 3-4 days.

We look forward to our long lasting.and cordial business relations with you based on open account with quarterly settlements.

Yours faithfully

Sin Wah Hin
Manager

SIX

COLLECTION LETTERS

Collection and realization of dues or over-due payments is not an easy task. Sometimes it becomes really exasperating, but it should never be expressed in your collection letters as far as possible. These letters should always be courteous, polite but firm and persuasive. Collection letters are written as reminders at intervals with increasing pressure and urgency till you have your dues collected. Each default in payment should be dealt on its merits because there might have been some genuine reasons behind late payment. It is not a good policy to doubt the intentions and integrity of buyers for late payments indiscriminateiy.

To make a bad debtor pay is not an easy task. It presupposes a lot of patience, perseverance and good skills in the supplier. The payer should be sent repeated reminders at regular intervals till you succeed in the realization of your payment. Sometimes you have to be quite hard with your bad-debtors but there cannot be any hard and fast rule. However, legal action should be avoided as far as possible, particularly when the money to be recovered is not very large.

1. *Supplier's Request for Payment*

TATHAGAT SUBSINGHE & SONS
205, Olcott Mawatha
Colombo-11 (Sri Lanka)

30 July, 19...

Telephone : 23814-8
Fax : 23873

Mr. Sangh Ratnam
Goldcraft Creations
423, De Mel Mawatha
Colombo-3 (Sri Lanka)

Dear Mr. Ratnam

Account No. 772/Invoice No. 4267

As per our records the above account of 20 April, 19... is now overdue for payment. This amount owing Rs. 10500.75 seems to have escaped your notice. We, therefore, request you to settle your account at your earliest.

However, in case the statement of account and invoice are found incorrect, or you may have any objection to raise, please feel free to let us know it immediately so that we may do our best to satisfy you.

We look forward to your early response and settlement of the account.

Yours faithfuly

M. Rantunge
Manager Finance

2. *First Reminder for Payment*

TATHAGAT SUBSINGHE & SONS
205, Olcott Mawatha
Colombo-11 (Sri Lanka)

Telephone : 23814-8
Fax : 23873

10 August, 19...

Mr. Sangh Ratnam
Gold Craft & Creations
423, De Mel Mawatha
Colombo-3 (Sri Lanka)

Dear Mr. Ratnam

We want to remind you that your account no. 772 for Rs. 10500.75 is overdue for payment. We sent you a letter on 10 July requesting you to settle this account at the earliest but to our great surprise, there has been no response.

We had granted you open-account facility on your request with quarterly settlement, but we have found that on many an occasion payment has fallen overdue and our requests and reminders for payment have met with no response. In return of granting you credit facilities and prompt execution of your orders we expect timely payment.

Please settle your account immediately by sending a cheque for Rs. 10,500.75 by return of post.

Yours faithfully

M. Rantunge
Manager Finance

3. *Second Reminder for Payment*

TATHAGAT SUBSINGHE & SONS
205, Olcott Mawatha
Colombo-11 (Sri Lanka)

Telephone : 23814-8
Fax : 23873

20 August, 19...

Mr. Sangh Ratnam
Gold Craft & Creations
423 De Mel Mawatha
Colombo-3 (Sri Lanka)

Dear Mr. Ratnam

We regret to say that our earlier two reminders asking for settlement of your account no. 772 for Rs. 10500.75, which has been long over due, have had no response.

Now, we shall be obliged to cancel your credit status in case you fail to settle your long overdue account within 10 days of the receipt of this letter.

We look forward to receive your cheque towards full settlement of the account at the earliest so that our cordial business relations are maintained.

Yours faithfully

M. Rantunge
Manager Finance

4. *Third Reminder for Payment*

TATHAGAT SUBSINGHE & SONS
205, Alcott Mawatha
Colombo-11 (Sri Lanka)

Telephone : 23814-8
Fax : 23873

20 August, 19...

Mr. Sangh Ratnam
Gold Craft & Creations
423 De Mel Mawatha
Colombo-3 (Sri Lanka)

Dear Mr. Ratnam

Subject : Payment of Statement of Account No. 772/ Invoice No. 4267 dated 20 April, 19...

We are really sorry to say that our earlier reminders to you requesting the payment of the above overdue account have met with no response.

Now, we cannot afford to wait any longer, to realize this money and therefore, insist that your account should immediately be settled, or we shall be obliged to pass on the matter to our legal counsellor at your risk and cost.

However, we do hope you will help avoid taking legal steps, which neither of us would like, by sending your cheque per return.

Yours faithfully

M. Rantunge
Manager Finance

GOLD CRAFT & CREATIONS
423 De Mel Mawatha
Colombo (Sri Lanka)

Telephone : 589316
Fax : 581745

5 September, 19...

Mr. M. Rantunge
Tathagat Subsinghe & Sons
205 Olcott Mawatha
Colombo-11 (Sri Lanka)

Dear Mr. Rantunge

I have received your earlier reminders about the settlement of our account no. 772 besides this one dated 1st September, but feel sorry that I could not reply because of circumstances beyond my control.

It is not through oversight that our account has not been settled so far and so long. In fact it was owing to my inability to collect my own outstanding amounting to a considerable sum of money because of recent unprecedented floods in some parts of the country. Now the situation has considerably improved and things are limping back to normal.

I am sure to receive a payment of big amount of money within this weeks. The payment is quite assured and reliable. Therefore, I shall settle the account as soon as I receive this payment although I am in urgent need of money for my own personal requirements. In the meanwhile please bear with me for some more days.

Yours faithfully

Singh Ratnam
Manager

6. *Buyer Explains Inability to Settle the Account*

GOLD CRAFT & CREATIONS
423, De Mel Mawatha
Colombo (Srilanka)

Telephone : 589316
Fax : 581745

7 September, 19...

Mr. M. Rantunge
Tathagat Subsinghe & Sons
205, Olcott Mawtha
Colombo-11 (Sri Lanka)

Dear Mr. Rantunge

I am sorry that so far and so long I have been unable to settle my account no. 772. As you might be aware that our premises were badly damaged in the ethnic violance that erupted in the beginning of the last month. In the explosion and violence some of our consignments due for despatch to our cash customers were destroyed. This unforeseen and unfortunate turn of events is the cause for non-payment of your overdue bills.

My claims are in the process of settlement with the insurance company and I am likely to receive the payment of compensation for lossess by the end of this month. Soon after I receive these payments, I shall settle my account.

I may tell you that my accounts with you have always been settled well in time and I never gave you a cause to complain before it. Now, it is with regret that I am obliged to write this explanation regarding my inability to settle the account in spite of your reminders. Please bear with me for some more time.

Yours faithfully

Sangh Ratnam
Manager

GOLD CRAFT & CREATIONS
423, De Mel Mawatha
Colombo (Srilanka)

Telephone : 589316
Fax: 581745

7 September, 19...

Mr. M. Rantunge
Tathagat Subsinghe & Sons
205, Olcott Mawtha
Colombo-11 (Sri Lanka)

Dear Mr. Rantunge

Further to your letter dated 1st September, 19... asking me to settle the account No. 772 for $ 10500.75, I enclose a cheque for $ 7000.00 only towards part payment of your statement of account. I shall remit the balance by the second week of the next month. Please bear with me until then.

As you are well aware, I have always been prompt in paying the bills except this time. I had bad luck and equally bad business. The sales have been very slack and slow during the past 5-6 months. I have not been able to sell even 25% of the goods received from you three months ago. But now there are signs of revival and the sales have begun to pick up.

Yours faithfully

Sangh Ratnam
Manager

Encl : as above

8. *Supplier's Reply to the above*

Dear Mr. Ratnam

Thanks for your letter of 10 September accompained by a cheque for $ 7000.00 only towards partial settlement of your overdue account.

My sympathies are with you and I appreciate your efforts to reduce the settlement amount, but regret to say that we cannot allow long term credit facilities. It is against our long established policy and practice. Therefore, we insist on receiving a further cheque for $ 3500.75 towards unpaid balance within 7 days.

We hope you will understand our problem and don't take it as unreasonable when we insist on immediate payment of the balance amount.

Yours sincerely

M. Rantunge
Manager

GOLD CRAFT & CREATIONS
423, De Mel Mawatha
Colombo (Srilanka)

Dear Rantunge

Further to your reminder of 4th September, 19... regarding settlement of my long over due account no. 772, I enclose a cheque for $ 10500.75 (Rupees ten thousand five hundred and paise seventy five only) in full settlement of account. I am really sorry and regret the delay in payment with due apologies.

The account remained unsettled on account of my long absence from the office because of some sudden and serious illness necessitating my hospitalization. As it was so sudden and unexpected, I could not instruct and authorise some one in the office to clear the account. I returned to the work today only.

As is clear the delay in payment of your bill has not been intentional at all. I hope this delay in payment has not caused you much inconvenience.

With thanks.

Yours faithfully

Sangh Ratnam
Manager

Encl : as above

10. *Buyer's Request to an Individual Customer for Payment*

NOVEL FURNISHING SDN BHD
Jalan Mega Mendung, Kuala Lumpur

Telephone : 03-781 3600
Fax : 03-782 0810

10 July, 19...

Mrs. Chia Soon Teck
29 Jalan Petaling
Kuala Lumpur

Dear Mrs Teck

On our checking the records we have discovered an amount of $ 70.00 outstanding on your account which is now over due for payment.

Please settle this over due account in full by return of post otherwise we shall be obliged to cancel your credit status and stop processing all your future order.

We look forward to receive your cheque within the next week towards settlement of the above account.

Yours faithfully

Edmund Yeo
Manager

29, Jalan Pealing
Kuala Lumpur

15 July, 19...

The Manager
Novel Furnhing Sdn. Bhd.
Jalan Mega Mendung
Kuala Lumpur

Dear Sir

I am in receipt of your letter dated 10 July, 19... asking me to settle my over due account amounting to $ 70. Your letter really surprises me because I have already despatched a cheque towards the full settlement of the account. The cheque dated 20 May, 19... was sent by ordinary post on 23 May, 19... for $ 70.00 only. The cheque was crossed and drawn on Grindlays Bank.

It seems the cheques got lost in the transit and did not reach you. Therefore, I am writing to the bank not to pay on it. However, I am enclosing a replacement cheque for the same amount, that is, $ 70.00.

This time I am sending the cheque with a bearer, Mr. Abdul Hamid our chauffeur to ensure that it reaches you immediately. Please acknowledge its receipt which could be sent through the bearer of this letter.

With thanks.

Yours sincerely

(Mrs.) Chia Soon Teck

Encl : as above

FRESHAIR SYSTEMS PTE LTD
Hougang Avenue, Singapore

Telephone : 385 0686
Fax : 366 2774

9 February, 19...

Mr. Hwee Lai
Kim Sen & Co.
Mountbatten Road
Singapore

Dear Mr. Lai

We thank you for your cheque for $ 125 only in partial payment of the long overdue account no. 947. The balance remaining due on your above account is now $ 600.00.

Since now you are in some financial difficulty and are not in a position to pay the balance amount due in near future requesting for extension of time to pay, we suggest that you pay it in four equal installments of $ 150.00 each. You may send your cheques by the end of every month beginning from March for three successive months. We hope it will suit you. So we expect your next cheque for $ 150.00 by the end of next month.

We understand your financial problems and appreciate your efforts to settle the account at the earliest. As, you are our old and reliable customer and so we suggest this scheme of payment in instalments.

Yours sincerely

Tom Lin
Manager

13. *Supplier Returns the Excess Amount*

SIAM STORES LIMITED
204, Siam Square
Bangkok (Thailand)

Telephone : 2516284
Fax : 2513812

10 November, 19...

Mr. Narapath Koman
7, Riverside Road
Bangkok

Dear Mr. Koman

Thank you for your letter of 5 November, 19... accompained by a cheque for Baht 11500.00 towards full settlement of your open account no. 725.

On checking we found that there was an error here in totalling in our bill and, therefore, we over-charged you by Baht 275.00. Thus, we have received Baht 275.00 in excess from you. We enclose a cheque for this amount to square up the account.

We regret the error in calculation and the consequent inconvenience caused to you. Please accept our apologies.

With thanks we look forward to your next order at an early date.

Yours sincerely

Thanarat Suphlong
Manager

14. *Supplier Offers Special Discount on Bill*

FRESHAIR SYSTEMS PTE LTD
Hongang Avenue, Singapore

Telephone : 385 0686
Fax : 366 2774

7 August, 19...

Mr. Heng Chan Hup
Max Electric Co.
Jalan Besar, Singapore

Dear Mr. Hup

Thank you for your order No. 1170 dated 1st August, 19... for 75 exhaust and 120 general deluxe fans listed in our catalogue at serial no. 8, 10 and 12. Really it is a pleasure to us to serve you, but there is so much rush of orders and pressure of work that we find ourselves unable to execute your order on urgent basis. However, we shall despatch these within 2-3 days and you will receive the delivery by the week end.

We may remind you that the payment of the previous bill no. 4376 of 20 July, 19... amounting to $ 1575.00 is due for payment on 30 October. However, in case if you can settle the account by 15 August, 19... you may avail of our special additional discount of 7% and deduct a sum of $ 110.25 and balance amount may be sent to us.

The bill for payment is enclosed in duplicate. The duplicate copy of it may be returned with the payment cheque.

We look forward to your immediate response and action in the matter.

Yours sincerely

Simon Wee
General Manager.

15. *Customer Sends the Bill for Correction*

MERRIAM & MERRIAM
279, Rizal Avenue
Manila (Philippines)

Telephone : 2387541
Fax : 632-2387982

9 July, 19...

Mr. Edward Marcos
Recto Mark
203, Vito Cruz Extension
Makati Manila, (Philippins)

Dear Mr. Marcos

I am sorry to return your bill for the month of June for revision and correction as the prices charged therein are higher by 5% than agreed with your sales representative when he called on me last time with samples. However, I thank you for prompt execution of my order.

The overcharges in the bill are really not justified and this might be because of an oversight. I therefore, request you to revise the enclosed bill accordingly and send me a fresh bill for payment. Unless the revised bill is sent, I am afraid your bill may remain unpaid and unsettled.

I look forward to your immediate response.

Yours faithfully

Julian Tan
Proprietor

16. Reply to the above

RECTO MARK
203, Vito Cruz Extension
Makati Manila (Philippines)

Telephone : 8123 879
Fax : 623-8123748

15 July 19...

Mr. Julian Tan
Merriam & Merriam
279 Rizal Avenue
Manila (Philippines)

Mr. Tan

Thank for your letter of 9 July, 19... asking us the correction and revision of our bill for June. In this bill we have charged at the current rate of prices and there is hardly any over-charging. According to our sales representative a trade discount of 17% was agreed on the prices given in our catalogue and pricelist. We have already allowed you same trade discount.

We may tell you that from tomorrow the prices of these items, already sent to you, will be revised upwardly. However, in this particular case we are willing to allow you 5% downward revision since you say that it was so agreed with our sales representative. As this is your first order, we have allowed this downward revision as a very special case. But we may tell you frankly that no such revision or correction in the bill will be allowed in future.

We are enclosing the revised bill in duplicate. Send the duplicate copy of the bill with the payment cheque. We look forward to your payment and fresh order.

Yours faithfully

Edward Marcos
Manager

Encl : as above

SEVEN

CIRCULAR AND NOTICES

1. *Circular Notifying Opening of a New Branch*

UNIQUE FABRIC PTE LTD
Bendemere Road, Singapore

Telephone : 291 8168
Fax : 293 1870
10 March, 19...

Dear Sir/Madam

We have pleasure in informing you that our new showroom at 40 Mac Pherson Road, Jackson Centre, Singapore, telephone no. 746 8100 (5 lines) has started functioning. In view of the growing popularity of our exclusive quality curtain and upholstery fabrics, this new showroom has been opened. This new and airconditioned showroom will make it easy for the people living in that area of the city to buy our state-of-the-art fabrics for curtains etc.

We have been providing the best possible services for the last several years, but we felt we could do still better by opening a new branch nearer to you so that service can be rendered to our customers more quickly.

Mr. Michael Mussa, with a long and excellent experience in the line, has been well-known to most of our customers. He has been appointed as the Manager of this new branch of ours. He will be pleased to receive and help you in making your selections whenever you drop in to make your purchases.

While the quality of the fabrics will always be the best, the prices will be reasonable since we purchase these items in bulk directly from the mills in Singapore and abroad.

We take this opportunity to thank you for your patronage and support and hope you would soon visit our new showroom to choose your requirement from our wide range of premium fabrics.

Yours faithfully
Yeo Song
Manager

2. *Circular about Clearance Sale*

LEAPIN LEATHER GOODS PTE LTD
Orchard Road, Singapore

Telephone : 733 6672
Fax : 733 4265

15 January, 19...

Dear Sir/Madam

As you are aware, like every year, our annual stock clearance sale begins from 20th January, 19... which will last for 15 days of the Lunar New Year festival.

A special attraction of this year's Lunar New Year stock clearance sale is that we have added a wide variety of genuine leather goods, a fascinating variety of leather footwear and shoes besides our usual ones.

In leather goods we offer belts, bags, brief cases, jackets, gloves and seminar items, all of best of quality leather.

As you might be aware our traditional leather footwear range includes specially designed fashion shoes for gents, ladies and children. Some of our leading popular brands are well-known for their super styling and uncompromising high quality.

Most of the stocks of our shoes are fresh and some of them are available at a bargain price.

Pay us an early visit and take advantage of the sale at incredible discount. For ladies and children there is a separate counter.

Yours faithfully

Munis Raza

3. *Circular Introducing a New Sales Representative*

APPOLLO AUTO PARTS (M) SDN BHD
Parsiaran Zaaba, Taman Tun. Ismail
Kuala Lumpur

Telephone : 03-718 0918
Fax : 603-719 7101

10 June, 19...

Dear Sir

We are pleased to introduce our new Sales Representative Mr. Van Foh. He is well qualified and experienced gentleman in the field of marketing and sales of auto-parts and engineering goods, and has represented a couple of reputed companies in this trade in the past 10 years. Recently he has joined us, and we are sure you will also extend him a hearty welcome like all of us here.

Next week he would start his trip of your part of the state and call on you any day during the next 10 days. During his stay in your town he will interview a number of other auto-dealers and companies. Please make his stay there as comfortable as possible.

We hope you will grant him an interview and send us through him a large order. We hope for far more improved and prosperous business between us in the years to come.

Yours faithfully

Mohmad Ibrahim
Manager Marketing

4. *Circular Announcing a New Partner*

GLOBE ENGINEERING SDN BHD
Hicom Damansasa Estate, Sek Syen
Shah Alam, Selangor

Telephone : 07-51 4506
Fax : 07-51 5406

18 Feb. 19...

Dear Sir

We feel extremely happy to announce that owing to tremendous expansion and integration of our business, we have taken Mr. Zainuddin Mohmad Dalib in our partnership. Our new partner has a long and extensive experience in this line. He is a businessman and a management expert and looks after day-today affairs of the company under the overall supervision and guidence of the Board of the Directors.

He holds a Masters degree in Engineering from Cambridge University, London and an MBA from University of Banaras, India. He is a past president of so many business and engineering associations and federations. He believes in result-oriented work and prompt modernisation to keep pace with the changing space and times. Besides, he brings in a large cash-investment urgently needed for our expansion, modernisation and acquisition of balancing equipment.

We thank you for your past confidence in us and hope for its continuance in future.

Yours faithfully

Rahman Ali
Managing Director

EIGHT

GOODWILL LETTERS

In the final analysis goodwill letters help a lot in promoting business. They create new business opportunities and strengthen the existing and old ones. They comprise letters of thanks, congratulations, appreciation, regret, sympathy, condolence, gratitude etc. These letters should be written as often as there are occasions for they go a long way in establishing and maintaining goodwill at a little cost and effort.

They should be written and sent promptly. They are appreciated by the recipients and in return bring good business. Goodwill letters should always be brief, to the point, sincere and friendly. They should be hand-written as far as possible because it gives a letter a touch of intimacy.

Sending out goodwill letters on appropriate occasions is one of the best ways to promote business and goodwill. These letters are bound to stand you in good stead in times of crisis, stress, strain, and cut-throat competition. Obviously they would result in appreciable increase in your business and profits.

1. *Congratulations on Moving to a Better and More Spacious Office-space*

WESTERN ENGINEERING CO PTE LTD
Jalan Jurong Kechil, Singapore

Telephone : 4611199
Fax : 462 2290

12 May, 19...

Dear Mr. Young

It was really a pleasant surprise to know just now about your change of office address. My heartiest congratulations on moving to a new and better office accommodation.

The new office location has great locational and business advantages as it is situated in the heart of the city and easily approachable from different areas of the city. This prime and prestigious location will go a long way in increasing your business many fold.

It was natural that you should have moved to such a spacious and advantageous premises since your business in refrigeration industry has recorded an excellent growth in recent months. Your foreign collaboration has helped you a lot in registering this phenomenal growth and handsome gains.

I wish you still better results and turnover in your business.

Yours sincerely

John Smith

2. *Letter of Condolence on the Death of an Employee*

NICE ELECTRICALS (M) SDN BHD
Jaln Cheras, Kuala Lumpur

Telephone : 03-930 4811

10 August, 19...

Dear Mrs Dai Xim

We all are deeply grieved to learn about the sudden and tragic demise of your beloved husband. He had been in our employ for the last three years as engineer and we always found him so industrious, sincere, cooperative and disciplined. In his death we have lost a good and great employee of ours. These are the feelings shared by all who had the opportunity to work with him here.

We know how distressed, lonely, and grieved you might be in this hour of tragic and irreparable loss of your dear husband. We shall feel favoured if we could do anything for you and your children now or in the future.

Please accept our heartfelt sympathy.

Yours sincerely

Yeo Tian Ho
Manager Personnel

3. *Letter of Condolence to a Buyer*

CHAMPION EQUIPMENT SDN BHD
Jalan Lima Chan Sowlin, Kuala Lumpur

Telephone : 03-2413104

7 January, 19...

Dear Mr. Mohmed Yusop

It is with profound sense of sorrow and shock that I learnt about your beloved wife's death. Still I cannot believe that she is no more. The tragic news is so sudden and stunning that one would hardly believe it.

May the Almighty grant you strength to bear this irreparable loss. I hope the memory of the happy days with so full of love spent with her all these years will comfort you in the days to come. Your loss and suffering are shared both by my wife and myself. Our deepest sympathies go out to you.

Please don't hesitate to communicate to me if there is anything I can do for you in this hour of gloom and distress.

Yours sincerely

Robert Paul

4. *Letter of Sympathy to a Business-friend*

SCIENTIFIC INSTRUMENTS (M) SDN BHD
Taman Melawati, Kuala Lumpur

Telephone : 03-298 4371
Fax : 03-292 0777

11 February, 19...

Dear Hock

I am really sorry to know that you have to close your branch-office at Selangor because of loss. You tried your best to effect a turn-around but it was not destined to be. Hence there was no alternative left with you except to close down your branch office there. To a great extent it is because your partner ditched you. It was never expected of him. But now it cannot be helped and so must be endured.

I pray that all your lossess to be recovered and your business to prosper abundently in the near future.

Yours sincerely

Young Khang Tong

FAREAST PLASTICS SDN BHD
Shah Alam, Salengor

Telephone : 03-559 2286
Fax : 03-559 5796

10 May, 19...

Dear Sir

We regret to the price-increase of our plastic products with immediate effect in view of the higher input, labour and power costs and devaluation of our currency in relation to foreign exchange. However, we have kept the rise in prices to the minimum possible. It ranges from 12 to 20%. We are enclosing the new catalogue and pricelist.

As you are aware the imported contents in the manufacture of our finished goods roughly amounts to 40% and there has been a steep increase in the prices of our imported raw material. Then there has been a sharp increase in overheads and transportation charges.

It deserves repetition that we have kept this rise to the minimum by economising in other areas like conservation of energy, manpower and by recycling of waste gases to produce power and energy.

We are sorry for this increase in prices but this is certainly not unreasonable and still on the lower side in comparison to the general increase in prices to about 30%.

Yours sincerely

Hwee Lai

6. *Letter of Thanks for Prompt Execution of an Order*

UNITED AUTO ENTERPRISES SDN BHD
Jalan Jambu Air Mawar
Kuala Lumpur

Telephone : 03-6273592

10 December, 19...

The Manager
Soong Auto Spares Pte. Ltd.
Singapore

Dear Sir

We thank you for your prompt execution of our order no. 437 of 1st December, 19... We are writing this note to express our happiness and thanks. This promptness in despatch and delivery of auto-parts has helped us a lot in keeping our clients and customers well satisfied. It has also helped us to widen our sales network.

We hope our orders in future will also receive the similar attention.

With thanks

Yours sincerely

Kheng Guan

7. *Letter of Thanks for First Order*

AIR SYSTEMS PTE LTD
Hougang Avenue, Singapore

Telephone : 385 0686
Fax : 366 2774

1 June, 19...

The Manager Sales
Ecko Pte. Ltd.
Singapore

Dear Mr. Seng

We thank you for your order for 90 heavy duty exhaust fans and 50 aircirculators. You must have already received our formal acknowledgement of your order no. 7721 dtd. 20 Dec., 19... Your consignment is ready for despatch which you will receive within this week.

This is just to inform you how pleased we are to have received your first order and thank you for it once again and assure you of best our cooperation always.

You will see that our heavy duty fans etc. become popular among your customers very soon because they are efficient, smooth running, durable, trouble free, reasonable in prices and have lower operating cost.

We hope our prompt supply of your orders would lead to a close and lasting business association for our mutual benefit.

Yours faithfully

Abdul Karim

NINE

AGENTS AND AGENCIES

1. *Letter Applying for an Agency*

PLZA ENTERPRISE PTE LTD
Leng Kee Road, Singapore

Telephone : 475 4557

12 August, 19...

The Manager
Meng Huat Works Pte. Ltd.
Queens Way
Singapore

Dear Sir

This has reference to your advertisement in the *Jakarta Post* of yesterday in connection with appointment of stockists and agents for your industrial fastners and all types of rivets.

We are already agents for two well-known manufacturers of rivets and industrial festeners and related items. But in recent days we had a number of enquiries for your products and therefore are interested in the agency of your industrial fasteners. As we have a good and long experience in distributing and marketing these products, we can develop a good market for your items. We have very good business contacts in this area of the city. Moreover, we have sufficiently large space and showroom to store and sell your products.

If you need, we can provide a couple of excellent trade and bank references.

We shall be glad to know your terms and conditions in order to get the distribution rights in this part of the city at the earliest.

Yours sincerely

Hee Theng Fong

2. *Letter Offering Agency Rights*

TELECOM HOLIDINGS PTE LTD
Sims Avenue, Singapore

Telephone : 743 5555
Fax : 743 1855

10 December, 19...

The Manager
Globe Electronics Pte. Ltd.
Duneran Road
Singapore

Dear Sir

We are in search of an active and energetic agent with well established contacts with buyers in the city to sell our most advanced and modern important cordless telephones, telephone systems and answering machines. We believe you are one such agent to sell our new generation telephone systems.

We take this opportunity of enclosing our pricelist and the trade terms for you and hope that the state-of-the-art features of our phones together with a wide network of after-sales service will inspire you to accept our offer of distributors in your area.

We choose to offer you the agency on the recommendations on one of our very reliable agents in Kuala Lumpur from whom you have been buying pushbutton phones.

You will see from the enclosed pricelist that the prices quoted by us compare favourably with those of other makes. Moreover, these items have many high tech features of international standard. Besides we offer you quite a handsome commission of 25% on the net sales.

We hope you will come forward and accept our offer of agency at the earliest.

Yours faithfully

Tan Swee Seng
Manager

3. *Acceptance of Sole Agency*

GLOBE ELECTRONICS PTE LTD
Commonwealth Lane, Singapore

Telephone : 778 8222
Fax : 778 7661

15 December, 19...

Mr. Tan Swee Seng
Manager
Telecom Holidays Pte.Ltd.
Sims Avenue
Singapore

Dear Mr. Tan

We thank you for your letter of 10th December, 19... offering us sole distribution rights of your phone-systems in this area of the city. We thank you for your trust and confidence in us and are pleased to accept your terms and conditions of sole-agency.

We have directed our bankers to despatch you a bankdraft of $ 20,000 as security deposit which you are likely to receive by day after tomorrow.

We are sending our initial order separately. The consignment may be sent immediately by your carrier. Also send promotional material etc. with the consignment.

With this acceptance of offer of sole-agency for your phone-systems in our part of the city, we look forward to a long and beneficial business relationship with you.

Yours sincerely

Tom Whitman
Manager

4. *Agent's Request for Increase in Commission*

SENG CHESONG GO PTE LTD
Middle Road, Enterprise House
Singapore

Telephone : 336 3244
Fax : 339 5844

16 March, 19...

The Manager
John Smith Corporation
Genting Road
Singapore

Dear Mr. John

You might be well aware that inspite of tremendous competition, we have been quite successful in popularising your cameras and accessories among and users in the city. Consequently there has been a very good growth in sales and corresponding in crease in profits. Marketing and popularising your photographic items has not been that much easy as was expected, and we had to exert our most to push your items across the city. For this purpose we had to increase our number of sales persons and representatives resulting in increasing our expenses.

Still we are not complacent and exerting our best to boost the sales further and soon you will see the results. But we would like you to share this increase in our expenses in the form of increased commission. Therefore, we think it quite reasonable to ask you for 2% increase in our commission with immediate effect.

We hope that you would appreciate our position and consider this request of modest rise in commission favourably.

Yours sincerely

Lim Ah Tong
Manager

5. *Letter Declining to Raise Commission*

JOHN SMITH CORPORATION
Genting Road, Singapore

Telephone : 745 0488
Fax : 747 2022

21 March, 19...

The Manager
Seng Chesong Co. Pte. Ltd.
Middle Road
Enterprise House
Singapore

Dear Mr. Lim

We thank you for your letter of 16th March, 19... and once again appreciate your efforts in making our cameras and accessories popular among the customers. We admit that there is tough competition and it requires a lot of efforts and determination to boost the sale of these items, but still we are unable to grant you the increase of 2% in your commission, at present.

We have given considerably thought and attention to your request and after due consideration we find it not justified. It is against our established policy to grant-rise in commission so soon. We don't want to set a bad precedent by agreeing to your request as it would render our normal business with our other sole agents and distributors difficult, if not impracticable.

We want to assure you of our full cooperation and consideration in the matter but it is not the right time to ask for an increase in commission.

Yours sincerely

John Smith
Manager

6. *Conditional Acceptance of an Offer for An Agency*

GOOD LIVING GRAND SDN BHD
Jalan Amany, Kuala Lumpur

Telephone : 03-618 7891
Fax : 03 618 6105

9 April, 19...

The Manager Marketing
Tuck Seng Hong Pte Ltd.
Coleman Street
Singapore

Dear Mr Osman Suleman

Thank you for your kind offer of agency to us for you solar cookers and heaters. You would be glad to know that I am favourably disposed to accept it.

However, I may point out at the very outset that solar cookers and heaters are totally new and inconventional items and people will not accept them easily. Therefore, we will have to extert maximum to sell these goods among the householders to whom the solar-cooking is totally a new and strange idea. We will have to demonstrate them the use of this unconventional items by going from door to door. It means a lot of extra efforts and expenditure is warranted and so we feel that your offer of 15% commission is too meagre.

Therefore, I am to request you to raise this commission to a reasonable amount of 25%. On the face of it, this may look on the higher side, but efforts and exertion needed to sell these totally new items fully justify it.

I, therefore, feel that if this condition is acceptable to you, we shall be more willing to place our initial order of 100 solar-cookers and heaters soon after hearing from you.

Yours sincerely

George Yung

TEN

BANKING CORRESPONDENCE

1. *Letter to a Bank to Open a Current Account*

HOPE CONSTRUCTION CO. LTD
Chancery Lane, Singapore

Telephone : 2546377
Fax : 254 7007

The Manager
Royal Trust Bank (Asia) Ltd.
Raffles Place, Shell Tower
Singapore

Dear Sir

We are glad to inform you that the Board of Directors of the Company has decided in its meeting held today to appoint your Bank as our Company's Banker. A certified copy of the resolution appointing the Royal Trust Bank branch at Shell Tower, Singapore, as the Hope Construction Company's Bankers together with specimen signatures of the Board-members, is enclosed. Also enclosed are the copies of the company's certificates of incorporation and to commence business. Our company now wishes to open a current account with your branch of the bank.

I, as the Chairman and Managing Director of the company has been authorised to sign on all cheques drawn on company's account.

The bearer of this letter and accompanying documents Mr. Jacob Jeffery, the assistant accountant of our company, may be given necessary forms for specimen signatures etc. So that the current account in our Company's name may be opened at the earliest.

With thanks

Yours sincerely

Mark Tan
Managing Director

2. *Letter Requesting to Stop Payment of a Cheque*

256 Lavender Street
Singapore

14 May, 19...

The Manager
Deutsche Bank (Asia Pacific) Ltd.
Treasury Building
Raffles Plaza
Singapore

Dear Sir

I hereby confirm my telephonic message to you in the morning today to stop the payment of a cheque, details of which are given as under:

Cheque no. 0007772295, dated 12th May, 19... issued by me in favour of the Manager, Kum Eng Kee Restaurant, Upper Thompson Road, Singapore for $ 1000.

Please advise me immediately how to do the needful in this respect.

Thanks.

Yours faithfully

Nobel Lee

3. *Letter to Bank Claiming Balance in the Account of a Deceased Customer*

10 February, 19...

20 Scotts Road
Singapore

The Manager
Deutsche Bank (Asia Pacific) Ltd.
Treasury Building
Raffles Plaza
Singapore

Dear Sir

It is with extreme sorrow that I have to inform you that my younger sister Lolita Donne died in a road accident on 30th January, 19... in Singapore while coming back home from her office in the evening. Since she was unmarried and not in a position to make a will, I being her only brother, am the legal claimnant to the balance amount lying to her credit in her savings account in your bank.

I therefore, request you to transfer that balance to my savings account no. 5796, in your bank. I am enclosing a copy of the police report as proof of her death. Also enclosed is the savings pass book account no. 57777 of my deceased sister. I am prepared to do whatever further formalities are required of me to be done in this regard.

Yours faithfully

John Donne

4. *Reply to the Claimant for Transferring the Balance of the Deceased Customers to his Account*

Deutsche Bank (Asia Pecific) Ltd.
Treasury Building, Raffles Plaza

15 February, 19...

Telephone : 321 6789
Fax : 224 0848

Mr. John Donne
20 Scotts Road
Singapore

Dear Mr. Donne

With reference to your application of 10th February, 19... we want to inform you that the balance amount standing to the credit of your deceased sister's Savings Account no. 5777 can be transferred to your Savings Account with this bank only after completion of certain formalities.

As such, you are welcome to call at our bank on any working day to enable us to help you in the matter.

Yours faithfully

J. Eliot
Manager

5. *Letter Reporting the Loss of a Locker Key*

21 May, 19...

21, Tempines Street
Singapore

Royal Trust Bank (Asia) Ltd.
Raffles Place
Sheel Tower
Singapore

Dear Sir

The locker no. 496 in your branch of the Bank stands in my name. The key of this locker has been lost somewhere during my bus journey from my residence to the office at 30, Bencoolen Street, Singapore last Friday, 20th May, 19... I have already reported this loss to the police and am enclosing a photocopy of the receipt of this report, but I would like you to take necessary precautionary measures so that no one may use the key for opening the locker unauthorisedly.

I would also request you to promptly get the locking mechanism of my locker changed with a new key.

Please advise me on the charges which I will be required to pay for getting the locking mechanism of my locker changed at your end.

Yours faithfully

Elizabath Tong

6. Letter to Bank Requesting Overdraft Facility

SEA-VIEW MAIDEN HOTEL
IBM Towers, Anson Road
Singapore

4 January, 19...

Telephone : 223 2155
Telex : Rs. 38744 AVI
Fax : 223 1673

The Manager
Royal Trust Bank (Asia) Ltd.
Raffles Place Sheel Tower
Singapore

Dear Sir

I am in urgent need of an overdraft on my hotel's account up to $ 130,000 for the period of 6 months from now.

As you are well aware, I have been one of your old customers with a current and savings accounts. The present balances in our accounts are $ 135,000 and $ 10,000 respectively. Last year I was allowed a similar overdraft facility for $ 80,000 against the title deeds and fixed assets of our hotel. I repaid the advance with interest within stipulated time.

I am willing to deposit with you the title deeds and fixed assets against this overdraft of $ 130,000 which I urgently require for the expansion of our hotel accommodation etc.

I shall be glad to call on you at your earliest convenience to discuss this matter with you personally.

Please treat the matter as urgent and reply immediately.

Yours faithfully

Simon Tsong
General Manager

7. *Reply to the above*

ROYAL TRUST BANK (ASIA) LTD
Raffles Place, Sheet Tower
Singapore

9 January, 19...

Telephone : 2249111
Fax : 2253809

The General Manager
Sea-View Maiden Hotel
IBM, Towers, Anson Road
Singapore

Dear Mr. Tsong

Thank you for your letter of 4th January, 19... requesting us for an overdraft facility for $ 130,000 for a period of 6 months from now.

We are ready to grant you this facility on your hotel's current account for $ 130,000 and for above mentioned period. We have fixed an appointment for you to meet me next Friday, 15th January, 19... at 2 p.m. for further discussion in the matter.

You are advised to bring with you the tittle deeds etc. on your fixed assets mentioned in your above cited letter

Yours faithfully

Tan Swee Seng
Manager

8. *Letter Informing a Customer about Expiry of an Overdraft Facility.*

THE NIKKO MERCHANT BANK LTD.
Battery Road, Singapore

Telephone : 223 3390
Fax : 225 2854

20 February, 19...

Mr. Chan Teck Fatt
Sophia Road
Singapore

Dear Sir

This is to inform you that the over-draft facility granted to you on your company's account is expiring on 28th February, 19... We shall appreciate if you would arrange to get the account closed in full on or before the above date. However, if you are interested in renewing this facility, kindly submit your application with the following documents/papers:

> Three certified copies of your company's balancesheet showing the profit and loss.

The balance sheet should have been duly audited by your authorised chartered accountants.

Please note that withdrawls will not be allowed in the account after the expiry of this overdraft facility.

Yours faithfully

Fredesic Lee
Manager

9. *Letter to a Customer Regarding Maintaining Minimum Balance in the Account*

Dear Sir

It has been observed on a review of our books that you have not been maintaining the prescribed minimum balance of $ 25 in your savings bank account no. 994602. As you are aware that every customer with the facility of withdrawls by cheques is required to maintain a minimum balance of $ 25.

Please, therefore, deposit the necessary amount to make it total $ 25, and also ensure that a shortfall like this is not repeated in future. We could have dishonoured your last cheque which caused this shortfall, but our consideration for you as our old and valuable customer did not allow us to do so. In return, we expect you to cooperate with us in the matter and do the needful without further delay.

Yours sincerely

Jacob Kia Bee
Manager

10. Letter Allowing Overdraft Facility to a Customer

THE NIKKO MERCHANT BANK LTD
Battery Road, Singapore

18 April, 19...

Telephone : 223 3390
Fax : 225 2854

Mr. Wong Chew Ho
45, Jurong East Street
Singapore

Dear Mr. Wong Chew Ho

This is with reference to your application of 10 April for an overdraft facility on your company's account. I am pleased to inform you that the Board of Management of our Bank has sanctioned you an overdraft facility limiting to $ 300,000 against hypothecation of stocks with our Clearing Agents. The stocks should be insured against fire, theft etc.

The amount carries an interest of 2½ percent over and above the bank rate to a minimum of 10 percent. This facility is granted to you on the full assurance and guarantee of Mr. Ahmed Sheriff of Endura Trading Co. Pte. Ltd. and is for the purpose of purchasing balancing equipment for your factory details of which you will have to furnish to the Bank when you buy it.

Please send a draft of a guarantee policy from Mr. Ahmed Sheriff, or request him to call on our bank on any working day to execute the guarantee so that we can proceed further in the matter soon.

I assure you of my best of service and cooperation ever.

Yours faithfully

Teck Hock Hin

CHAPTER ELEVEN

INSURANCE CORRESPONDENCE

1. *Letter Asking Insurance Rates*

12, Napier Road
Singapore

7 March, 19...

The Manager
Cosmic Insurance Corpn. Ltd.
Cosmic Insurance Building
North Bridge Road
Singapore

Dear Sir

We intend to despatch a heavy consignment of bonded cargo valued at $ 3,000 by a road transport carrier of Asia Transport Service (S) Pte. Ltd. 10, New Bridge Road, Singapore to Kuala Lumpur sometimes next week.

The cargo is to be delivered at 16, Jalan Empat, Kuala Lumpur. We want to cover this consignment against all risks from our above address to Kuala Lumpur. Would you please quote your rate for the cover at the earliest.

Yours faithfully

Hong Giap Sun

2. *Letter Asking for Life Insurance*

5 January, 19...

41 Block
Serengoon Central
Singapore

The Manager
First Capital Insurance Ltd.
Bai Building, Robinson Road
Singapore

Dear Sir

My wife, my daughter and I, aged 30 years, 8 years and 35 years respectively, are interested in getting ourselves insured for life. I shall feel obliged if you send your agent with necessary proposal forms etc. required for the purpose on any day to his convenience in the afternoon.

I look forward to your agent on an earlier date.

Yours faithfully

Haip Lee

3. *Reply to the above*

FIRST CAPITAL INSURANCE LTD.
Bai Building, Robinson Road
Singapore

Telephone : 222 2311
Fax : 1800 222 3547

10 January, 19...

Dear Mr. Haip Lee

We thank you for your letter of 5 January 19... requesting us to send our agent to help you in obtaining life insurance cover for your wife, daughter and yourself.

In this regard, we want to inform you that our agent Mr. Michael Wah Hin will call on you on Tuesday, the 15th of January at 2.30 p.m. to help you fill up the necessary proposal forms. He would also let you know in detail about the different life policies available with us.

Meanwhile we are enclosing printed material to help you to have a general idea about life insurance and its different policies.

We look forward to provide you soon with required insurance for life.

With thanks.

Yours faithfully

Ng Kim Seng
Manager

4. *Follow-up letter Accepting Insurance*

20 January, 19...

41 Block
Serengoon Central
Singapore

The Manager
First Capital Insurance Ltd.
Bai Building, Robinson Road
Singapore

Dear Mr. Ng Kim Seng

With reference to your agent Mr. Michael Wah Hin's visit on 15th January, 19.. we have decided to accept the insurance for my wife, daughter and myself.

The required proposal forms duly filled in and signed along with relevant cheques towards payments of premium of first instalments are enclosed. I hope you will find the forms .etc. in order. We could have completed all these formalities on that very day of your agent's visit but we could not do so for the absence of my wife who had been out on an urgent work.

Kindly acknowledge the receipt of first premiums and acceptance of the proposals at the earliest.

With thanks

Yours faithfully

Hiap Lee

5. *Letter to an Insurance Company Seeking Information about Surrender Value of a Policy*

8 January, 19...

9 Upper Circular Road
Singapore

The Manager
Zurich Insurance (Singapore)
Robinson Towers
Robinson Road
Singapore

Dear Sir

I have an insurance with you for $ 39000 vide my endowment policy no. 74320 since 1 January, 19...

I have been paying annual instalments towards it for the last 7 years, but now I want to surrender it because I am in urgent need of money for purchase of a house.

Would you please quote its present surrender value so that I may proceed further in the matter.

I look forward to hearing from you soon.

With thanks

Yours sincerely

Lim Chim Leong

6. *Letter to an Insurance Company for Settling Claims on Husband's Death*

12 Depot Lane
Singapore

10 July, 19...

The Manager
Zurich Insurance (Singapore)
Robinson Towers
Robinson Road
Singapore

Dear Sir

It is with much grief and sorrow that I have to report about my husband Mr. Abdul Karim's death. He died of a massive heart attack in the hospital on 5th July, 19... He was insured with you for $ 50,000 vide policy no. 0071297. I am his sole legal nominee. Moreover, I am the sole executor and legatee by his will executed sometimes back.

I enclose the certified copies of death certificates, statement of his will and other documents for your perusal and verification. I shall produce the original documents when required. The claims due following my husband's death may please be settled at the earliest as I am in dire need of money to meet my personal expenses.

I look forward to hearing from you soon.

Yours faithfully

(Mrs.) Abdul Karim

7. *Letter to an Insurance Company about Increase in Cover*

101 Block
Queen's Street
Singapore

10 March, 19...

The Manager
Zurich Insurance (Singapore)
Robinson Towers
Robinson Road
Singapore

Dear Sir

I have with you a comprehensive policy no. 992275 for my imported luxury car M-Benz. The renewal of the policy is due next month. But I want to increase the amount of insurance cover of my car from $ 150,000 to $ 160,000 with effect from the next month when the renewal of the policy is due.

Therefore, would you please let me know the increase in premium in accordance with the increase in the amount of cover of my above noted car from the date of next renewal?

I look forward to your early reply.

Yours faithfully

(Dr.) Ng Kim Seng

8. *Letter to an Insurance Company about Tour Insurance*

20 March, 19... 107, Cecil Street
Singapore

The Manager
Cosmic Insurance Corpn. Ltd.
Cosmic Insurance Building
North Bridge Road
Singapore

Dear Sir

I shall be on one and half months long tour to Malaysia with my family in my Toyota car.

The car is already insured with you for $ 60,000 under comprehensive policy no. 346907 dtd. 9 July, 19.. Now, I want to have an all risk policy to cover loss and damage to our baggage and other personal properties like video camera, binoculars, suitcases, jewellery, money, traveller's cheques etc.

I would very much appreciate if you would send the details of your terms and conditions on which you could issue such a cover.

I look forward to your immediate response as I want to proceed on this tour as soon as possible. If you so desire, you may send your representative for discussion and execution on any day at your convenience at the earliest But better if he fixes an appointment with me over phone. My phone number is 272 8922.

Yours faithfully

Khoo Seng Hai

TWELVE

APPLICATION FOR APPOINTMENTS

Business means buying and selling of goods or services. An application for a job is basically an attempt to sell one's services to a prospective employer. It helps you to secure a job of your choice. Thus it is a sales letter and so should have all the qualities of a good and meaningful sales letter. It should be well planned and well written so as to persuade the employer to invite you for an interview leading to your appointment. In other words, getting a job requires salesmanship of a very high order. A candidate applying for a job can be described both as a salesman and a commodity for sale.

The main object of an application for a job is to arouse the prospective employer's interest in your skills and abilities. The employer should feel, while going through your application, that it is worthwhile to engage your services. Your object should be to urge him to call you for an interview and then to offer you the position advertised.

A good application may not ensure you a job, but it may certainly ensure a chance for an interview. But it all depends on how you draft your letter of application. Further your selection depends on how you fare in the interview in the competition with other applicants. Therefore, give all the relevant details of your educational qualifications, experience etc. in your application in such a manner that it motivates the prospective employer to call you for an interview. Make your application distinctive by highlighting the various points of advantage that make you a better choice than other applicants.

Let your application be neat and clean, written or typed on a good quality paper, preferably typed unless it is required that it should be in your own hand-writing. A well-typed letter of application is attractive, easy to read and will create a good impression leading to winning of the employer's interest and confidence. And since there are no two identical situations, every application should be originally framed and typed to suit the requirements of a particular job.

1. *Application for the Post of an Accounts Clerk*

7, January, 19...

21, Puyat Avenue
Manila

The Manager
Native Industries
29, Pinoneer street
Manda Luyong
Metro Manila, (Philippines)

Sir

Being given to understand that there lies a vacany for the post of Accounts Clerk in your company, I humbly submit my candidature for the same. I have given below my detailed biodata for your kind consideration:

I am a B.Com. graduate with high second division with first division marks in Accountancy and Book-keeping.

I have 2 years of experience as an accounts clerk that I worked with Nirandra & Sons, 29 N. Rays. Street, Manila. As I am good at arithmetic and have good handwriting, I was entrusted with leadger-keeping job. My superiors were highly satisfied with my work and conduct. However, I had to leave this job on account of some family circumstances.

For the last six months I have been working as an accounts clerk with a reputed business firm but my appointment here is purely temporary against a leave vacancy, so I am obliged to seek a permanent job. My present employers would be glad to be my referee and it is with their consent and knowledge that I apply for this post.

I am a young man of 22 years with good health and neat working habits. I have a good family background. If I am given a chance to work under you, I am confident to win your appreciation through my hard work and sincerity.

I look forward to an early response and interview letter.

With thanks

Yours faithfully

Bernard Benson

2. *Application for the Post of Medical Representative*

15, Thonburi Street
Bangkok

9 July, 19....

The Manager
Pattaya Medical Hall
39, Naravan Street
Bangkok

Dear Sir

With reference to your advertisement for the position of a Medical Representative in today's *Bangkok Times*, I would like to apply for this post.

I have seven years experience in this line as I have been selling drugs, medicines and other pharmaceutical products in the city and neighbouring areas. I have wide and lasting business contacts with chemists, druggists, doctors and medical practioners here and in other towns. At present, I represent a reputed pharmaceutical company manufacturing tablets, capsules, syrups and many other vital medicines. I am satisfied with my work here, but feel that your company is offering me better financial and career opportunity, and therefore, I seek this change.

Mr. Sutha Koman, my Managing Director has gladly consented to provide reference for me. If you require, I would give further details about him and the company I am serving at present, at the time of interview. I shall be happy to provide you more references and information if you need.

It may also be mentioned that medical salesmanship is in my interest for I was initiated in this profession by my late father who himself was a well-known salesman of medicines and chemicals. In addition to my educational qualification and experience, I think my family tradition in medical salesmanship might further qualify me for this position.

I am a science graduate with distinction in Chemistry. I have also done a course in medical salesmanship and advertising. I am 31 years of age and still a bachelor. I fully enjoy travelling as a salesman and have an aptitude for result-oriented jobs. There is a lot of professional drive, initiative and acumen in me which make me so eager to be affiliated with a firm like yours which can offer me a future matching my energies, ambition and skills.

I look forward to an early response and opportunity for an interview.

Yours sincerely

Richard Toh

3. *Application for the Post of a Typist Clerk*

12 April, 19...

Shyam Niwas
Bousbon Street
Port Louis

The Manager
Robert & Harry
12/82, Central Market
Port Louis
(Mauritius)

Dear Sir

I want to apply for the post of a Typist Clerk, advertised in the *Mauritius Times* of 23 January, 19....

I am a young man of 20 years of age with sound health and active habits. As for my qualification is concerned, I am an arts graduate I graduated year before last with first class marks in Economics securing 55% in aggregate.

I have also done a certificate course in shorthand and typing. My speed in shorthand and typing is 80 and 40 words a minute respectively.

At present I am employed with a small engineering firm as a typist and my work involves much of tabulation and figure work besides usual running matter. Before this I worked for about 4 months as a part-time typist with a lawyer.

My present employer is quite satisfied with my work conduct and does appreciate these, but I feel the post you offer has better chances for my capacity and capability. My present employer will be glad to give a reference for me.

If I am appointed to the post, I shall do my best to give you entire satisfaction.

Yours faithfully

Ram Gulam Joshi

4. *Application for the Post of a Counter Sales-girl.*

9 Bagh Bazar
Kathmandu

3 June, 19...

The Manager
Himalayan Trading Centre
Red Cross Building
Thapathali
Kathmandu (Nepal)

Dear Sir

My friend Ms. Kiran Bala Thapa, who is a counter sales-girl at your company's show-room has told me that she intends to leave her job soon as she is going to be married soon to a gentleman in Sikkim. She has told me that working under you was quite fruitful and rewarding. I would request you now to consider me for this post in her place.

I am a graduate from Benaras Hindu University, India and have some experience in the line. Soon after my graduation I worked as a sales girl at a reputed Sari-shop in Benaras for about six months, but then I had to leave the job and come here to help my ailing mother and old father. I also know typing and can handle correspondence.

I would be thankful if I am given a chance to serve you in the place of my friend Kiran Bala Thapa. You may enquire from her about my good habits and hard-working nature and excellent conduct.

I look forward to your early response.

Yours faithfully

Śaroj Kulshrestha

5. *Application for the Post of a Lady Telephone Operator*

37, Dam Street
Colombo-12
10 August, 19.....

The Manager
Pacific Cooperative
14, Devnampiyatissa Road
Masidana
Colombo-10
(Sri Lanka)

Dear Sir

I want to apply for the post of a lady Telephone Operator advertised in today's *Sri Lanka Express*, an opportunity that I have just been looking for, because my services have been retrenched from Messers All Ceylon Co., Colombo as they have closed down their business here and have shifted to Kandy.

Soon after my certificate course in telephone-operation, I joined Messers All Ceylon Co. in 19... Since then I had been working for this firm for almost 2 years before this retrenchment. I controlled 21 extensions. My employers were very much satisfied with my work and had given me one advance increment. They wanted me to join them at Kandy. But my family circumstances do not permit me to move out of Colombo.

I am enclosing a testimonial and appreciation letter from my employers and they would be really pleased to provide you my reference.

As for my basic educational qualification, I am a graduate and have a good command over written and spoken English, Sinhala and Tamil. I am a young lady of 21 with sound health, excellent working habits and pleasing personality and am unmarried.

If you consider me for this post, I would feel obliged.

Yours faithfully

Buddapriya Ransinghe

6. *Application for the Post of a Food Technologist*

3 March, 19... 211, Jalan Sultan
Jakarta

The Manager
Food & Inns Service
24, Jalan Gunding
Jakarta, (Indondesia)

Dear Sir

I would like to be considered for the post of a Food Technologist in your company advertised in yesterday's *Jakarta Times.*

I hope my qualification and 6 years of long experience in product development along with administrative experience in Research and Development setup, make me a suitable candidate for the above mentioned post.

I would like to take up this post as it is more challenging and has far better opportunities to suit my skills, abilities, aptitude and experience in the line. My expertise and experience in the field to food and turning food concepts into actual formulations have little scope here. Moreover, you are offering far better remuneration keeping with my aspirations and industry standards.

I am B. Tech. in Food Technology and have been working in a local company producing a couple of brand food products for the last 5 years to the full satisfaction of my employers and superiors. But of late I am not feeling the desired job satisfaction here. During my working here I have been instrumental in the development of a few very successful food formulations now popular among the consumers. I believe in result-oriented and challenging opportunities and, therefore, I seek this change.

I would be greatful if I could have the opportunity to discuss my credentials and remuneration in detail personally at the time of interview at your earliest convenience.

Yours faithfully

S. Subandrio

7. *Application for the Post of a Steno-typist*

Mauritius

12 September, 19....

The Manager
Jupiter Traders
2, Club Road
Vacaos
(Mauritius)

Sir

Being given to understand that a post of Steno-typist has been lying vacant under you, I wish to apply for the post.

I am a commerce graduate with honour in Economics. After doing my graduation last year, I have undergone a 9 months training course in typewriting and shorthand at Pitman's Training College, Port-Louis. My present speed in typewriting and shorthand is 40 words and 80 words per minute respectively.

For the last 3 months I have been working with a practising lawyer on daily payment basis. Here I take down dictation and then transcribe it. I also look after my lawyer's correspondence independently.

I am a young man of 21 years with very sound health, clean working habits and aptitude for hard work. I am very much interested in seeking this change as my present job is purely temporary on daily payment basis and not so satisfying.

My present employer is fully satisfied with my work and conduct and has full sympathy with my desire to improve my prospects by joining your firm. He would be glad to give reference for me.

I look forward to hearing from you soon.

Yours faithfully

Naresh Chandra

8. *Application for the Post of Manager Bulk Drugs*

12, Up Thomson Road
Singapore

9 October, 19....

The Manager Personnel
Life Pharmaceutical Ltd.
11, Jalan Bukti
Singapore-2158

Dear Sir

I have come to know through a reliable source that you are in urgent need of a Manager who can work successfully to your entire satisfaction in your bulk drugs section. I request that I would be considered for this post.

At present I have been working as a Deputy Manager in a bulk drug manufacturing company for the last 4 years and am responsible for fine chemicals production in the plant. My operational areas include production, planning, coordination of the batch activities, quality control and quantity of the output, shop-floor management, cost controi etc. I am a graduate in Chemical Engineering and a post-graduate in Organic Chemistry.

The post offered by you is really attractive as it offers better utilisation of my expertise and abilities. A copy of my curriculum vitae is enclosed giving further details of my qualifications, work experience etc.

I hope you would provide me an early opportunity to present myself at an interview.

Yours faithfully

George Mathews

9. *Application for the Post of an Accounts Officer*

Jakarta
(Indonesia)

20 May, 19...

The General Manager
Three Brothers Company
29, Jakarta Road
Bali (Indonesia)

Dear Sir

I found your advertisement in the *Jakarta Times* of yesterday for the post of an Accounts Officer. As I am quite interested in the post, I would like to apply for the same.

I have over 5 years long experience as Deputy Accounts Officer in a reputed financial firm here. My experience relates to financial matters, taxation and dealings with national and foreign financial institutions.

The enclosed curriculum vitae will provide you details regarding my excellent performance and track record in the profession. I am willing to negotiate competitive and satisfying remuneration package.

My present Managing Director and Manager Personnel would be glad to provide references for me.

I shall be glad to provide you any further information you may need at the time of interview. I look forward to an early letter of interview.

Yours sincerely

P.S. Sukarno

10. *Application for the Post of Private Secretary*

12, India Street
Port Louis
(Mauritius)

2 January, 19...

The Manager
Golden Cross Associates
2, Bourdon Street
Port Louis (Mauritius)

Dear Mr. Sameer Ranjan

For the last 6 years I have been working as a Senior Stenographer with the standard Mart Ltd. Stanley Rose Bud, Mauritius. Of late I have been looking for a change of employment which would widen my experience and improve my prospects. I have been told by a very senior person working in your organisation that you need an efficient private secretary and, therefore, I would like to apply for this post with the hope that such a large and reputed organisation like yours would be able to use my service in a far better way.

My responsibilities here as a Senior Stenographer to the General Manager include taking dictation, transcription, supervising junior staff and dealing with correspondence independently.

I would welcome the opportunity to work under you as your Personal Secretary and would satisfy you with my hard and sincere work. I am 23 years young and enjoying excellent health. My present employers are well pleased with my accurate faultless work, punctuality, clean work habits and conduct and would be glad to testify these if needed. I am also familiar with attending and taking minutes of meetings and interviews and receiving the visitors. I have an excellent command over English, Hindi and Creole and can read, write and speak these languages. Hindi is my mother-tongue. My present speed in typing and shorthand is 50 and 100 words per minute respectively.

I hope to receive an interview letter soon so that I may present further details in respect of my experience, qualifications etc.

Yours faithfully

Nidhi Lakhanpal

11. *Application for the Post of a Sales Organizer*

Yaowaraj Street
Bangkok-10100

3 March, 19....

The Personal Manager
Asian Cooperatives
14, Sukhmvit Road
Bangkok-50141, (Thailand)

Dear Sir

Your advertisement in today's *Bangkok Times* for the post of a Sales Organizer has fascinated me and, therefore, I wish that I would be considered for the post in view of the following facts and details.

I am a Commerce graduate with first division and also possess a diploma in Business Administration with specialisation in Sales Organization.

I have been working in a reputed electrodes (graphite) manufacturing company here for the last 2 years as an Assistant Sales Organizer. Before this I worked as a travelling salesman for 3 years for a company making mattresses and rubber items for use in household.

I am 30 years of age with sound health and aptitude for challenging opportunities. I am fully conversant with market research and investigation besides I have good contacts and influence with bulk and retail buyers in the city.

I hope to receive an early response and interview letter.

Yours sincerely

Sukirti Rai

12. *Application for the Post of a Trading Manager*

Colombo

9 April, 19.....

The General Manager
All Ceylon Distribeitors
12/1, Classen Place
Colombo-5
(Sri Lanka)

Dear Mr. Vijaya Surya

I understand that you are in need of the services of an experienced and well qualified Trading Manager. I hope the following details may adequately meet the requirements of your office job vacancy.

I am B. Com. (Hons.) from the Delhi University with specialisation in Accounting and Auditing. I also possess diploma in Business Administration from the University of Sri Lanka with 70% aggregate marks. Recently I have appeared in the final examination of the Institute of Cost and Works Accountant, Colombo after completion of Intermediate Examination of the above Institute. The result of the Final Examination is awaited.

I have 5 years of intensive experience in the procurement and export of industrial products particularly chemicals and animal feeds as I have been working as an Assistant Manager Sales and Trading for the last 5 years with a reputed local trading company having an annual turnover of US$ 100 million. My other duties here include supervision of accounts and finances. I am also familiar with overseas markets, particularly those of the Middle East and the South-East Asia.

I recently attended a month long Orientation Programme related to Development and Execution of Trade.

I am fluent in Hindi, Sinhala, Tamil, English and Arabic languages. At present I am being paid Rs. 9,000 per month besides other allowances. I hope the salary offered for the post shall be commensurate with my qualifications and experience. However, it is negotiable and there cannot be any pre-condition in the matter. It may be mentioned here that I would require at least 2 months notice period before I resign the present post and join the new one in your organisation.

I would be glad to discuss with you in person further details at an early date. I hope to hear from you.

Yours sincerely

Jayant Ransinghe

SHANKHA & SHANKHA
281, Dam Street, Colombo

Telephone : 434682
Fax : 434721

29 July, 19...

The Manager
Regency Agency (Pvt.) Ltd.
109/110, Upper Ground Floor
Central Super Market Complex
Reclamation Road
Colombo-11, (Sri Lanka)

Dear Sir

We are considering Mr. S. Rantunge for the post of Senior Manager Design and Development in our company. The job involves design support of existing products and to develop modified and new products to meet customer's needs. It also involves coordination with various departments with references to international quality certification.

Mr. Rantunge has given your name as a reference while applying for this post. I would be most obliged if you can giveforth your frank opinion about his skills, abilities, and experience about designing, development and modifications of engineering tools etc. I understand that he worked in your company for about 5 years from 19... to 19...

I would like to know whether his services with you have been fully satisfactory and result-oriented, and whether you consider him fit and qualified for the present responsibilities in a large organisation like ours.

The information given will be treated strictly confidential. I am enclosing a stamped and self-addressed envelope for your convenience.

Yours faithfully

Bhaskar Rao
General Manager

14. *A Favourable Reply to the above*

REGENCY AGENCY (PVT) LTD
109/110, Central Super Market Complex
Reclamation Road, Colombo-11

Telephone : 4462831
Fax : 448316

7 August, 19...

The General Manager
Shankha & Shankha
281, Dam Street
Colombo-12

Dear Mr. Rao

I reply to your request of 29 July, 19... for a reference, I am glad to supply it favourably.

Mr. S. Rantunge's conduct and services with us have been entirely satisfactory. He has been in our employ for 3 years from July 19... till date. He is fully qualified and experienced in shouldering the responsibilities of a Senior Manager Design and Development in a large establishment like yours.

He is a graduate in Mech. Engg. and well conversant with latest tool designing techniques. I hope his long experience would stand him in good stead in this new and far more responsible capacity. I have no doubt about his fine conduct, sincerity to work and skills to face new job challenges. In my opinion he will prove an asset to your company on the core post. I wish him all success, but feel sorry to lose him.

Yours faithfully

Amitabh Senanayke

15. *Another Letter Requesting a Reference*

USA IMPORTS & EXPORTS CO
12, Queens Road, Hongkong

Telephone : 2731854
Fax : 2728964

7 April, 19...

The Personnel Manager
Wash & Kelley
2, Ferry Road
Hongkong

Dear Mr. James Taylor

Mr. B. Harvey has applied to us for the post of President Software Exports in our company. As you are aware this post involves full responsibility for the management of the company's international software export operations with major emphasis on project planning, testing and quality control. He will have to interact closely with the marketing and software development team to deliver projects on time and within estimates.

We actually need a suitable and experienced person with a degree in computer sciences and a diploma in management from a reputed institution in the country or abroad.

He has given your name as a reference stating that he is in your employment as Vice Presidents Exports. I shall be grateful if you will provide us information in strict confidence about his qualifications, experience, competence and conduct. I am enclosing a stamped and self-addressed envelop for your convenience.

Yours sincerely

Robert Joyce

16. A Letter of Recommendation

CRATIVE CRAFTS LTD
85-86, Cheapride, London-EC2V 6AA

Telephone : 071-242-2177/8

15 March, 19...

The Manager Personnel
Footguard Productions Ltd.
8, Discoll House, 17 Southampton Street
London, WC2E

Dear Mr. Picton

We are pleased to provide the information that you requested for concerning Ms. Rosalind Soros, with an understanding that it would be treated in strict confidence.

Ms. Soros has been with us for about three and a half years as Secretary. She is really a fine woman and a capable secretary with her qualities of both head and heart. She is sincere, efficient and intelligent. We have no hesitation in recommending her to serve in your organization.

I really regret the circumstances that led her to leave us. Our inability to grant her immediate promotion and substantial rise in her salary has compelled her to change her employer.

Yours sincerely

Keith Arnold
General Manager

17. Another Letter of Recommendation

CHAO MARKETING
231, Nathan Road, Kowloon
(Hongkong)

Telephone : 4873218
Fax : 5321489

21 January, 19...

The General Manager
Charles Lambart & Co.
29, Gaylord Road
Kowloon, (Hongkong)

Dear Mr. Long

I take this opportunity of responding to your letter of reference about Mr. Wong Shee Fun who has applied for the post of Product Manager. I feel pleasure in recommending him for this very senior and responsible post.

Though Mr. Fun has never been in our company but I know him thoroughly for the last several years as a very hard working and sincere officer. With his long experience, expertise and exceptional qualifications, I am sure he would be in a position to provide support, services and leadership to your sales team. His experience in the marketing of value-added consumer durables and white goods is an added advantage.

I hope his joining your company would prove a rewarding experience for both the company and Mr. Fun. I can recommend him to you with much confidence.

Yours sincerely

Teck Hock Hin

18. *A Testimonial*

MECKNZIE AGENCIES
292, Prince Edward Road
Kowloon (Hongkong)

Telephone : 2387651
Fax : 5432894

To Whom It May Concern

I have known Mr. Judith Novel for 5 years and have always found her most pleasant, hard working and trustworthy employee.

During this period she held position of increasing responsibility progressing from a Typist to my Personal Secretary. She was expert in organising meetings and got on well with people. As my Personal Secretary, she has been involved in correspondence, taking dictation and transcription, attending telephone and visitors and supervising the work of the juniors. Her work has always been systematic and meticulous. With her high standard of work and ready cooperation, she has endeared herself with all of us here.

It is with much regret that I have accepted her resignation to seek better prospects and benefits with a larger organisation.

I wish her all the best.

Hensy Jones
General Manager

23 September, 19...

19. Letter of Thanks to a Referee

16 Block, Martin Road
Singapore

12 June, 19...

The Manager
Royal Trust Bank (Asia) Ltd.
Raffles Place, Shall Towar
Singapore

Dear Mr. Tong

It is to thank you from the bottom of my heart for giving so favourable a reference and recommendation in support of my application for the post of a Chief Executive at Cosmic Insurance Corpn. Ltd., Singapore.

I hereby express my deep gratitude and appreciation for the generous help you gave in getting me this core post in such a large organisation. Your help and guidance have always inspired me to do my utmost best.

I once again express my thanks and gratitude for the reference you provided for me.

Yours sincerely

Chang Kia Bee

20. *A Letter Inviting for an Interview*

ROYAL INDUSTRIES LTD
129, Stadium Road, Dhaka (Bangladesh)

Telephone : 247381

9 March, 19...

Dear Ms. Gulshan Narseen

It is in response to your application for the post of a Stenographer in our establishment. We have shortlisted the candidates to be interviewed for the post and you are one of them. You are invited to attend the interview with Mrs Abida Khan, Manager Personnel, on Monday the 18th March, 19..... at 10.00 a.m.

Would you please let me know whether this date and time suits you?

Yours faithfully

Akram Hussain
General Manager

21. *Letter Confirming Attendence for Interview*

7 Nazrul Square
Dhaka

15 March, 19...

The General Manager
Royal Industries Ltd
129, Stadium Road
Dhaka

Dear Sir

Thank you for your letter of 9th March, 19.... inviting me to attend the interview on Monday the 18th March, 19... at 10.00 a.m. with Mrs Abida Khan, Manager Personnel.

I shall be glad to attend the interview at the above stated date and time. I look forward to meet Mrs Abida Khan.

Yours faithfully

Gulshan Nasreen

22. *An Appointment Letter*

HIMALAYAN TRADING CENTRE
Red-Cross Building, Bagh Bazar
Kathmandu (Nepal)

Telephone : 224192

2 February, 19...

Dear Mr. Nar Bahadur Thapa

Thank you for attending the interview on 3rd January, 19... The selection committee has decided to offer you the post of a Travelling Salesman on the starting salary of Rs. 3000.00 plus usual travelling and other allowances. Besides, you will also get a commission of 3% on all orders booked by you.

You are required to join by 15th of March, 19... failing which your appointment will be cancelled without any further intimation. No extension of joining time is permissible on any account. You will be entitled for 15 days paid holiday every year.

Please confirm in writing immediately that you accept this appointment on these terms and conditions, and that you will join your duties within the stipulated time.

Yours faithfully

Veer Bahadur Singh
Manager

23. *Letter Accepting the Employment*

77, Durbar, Lane
Kathmandu

5 Febraury, 19...

The Manager
Himalaya Trading Centre
Red-Cross Building
Bagh Bazar
Kathmandu (Nepal)

Dear Mr. Singh

Thank you so much for your letter of 2 February, 19... offering me the post of Travelling Salesman in your company.

I am glad to accept the post on the terms and conditions mentioned in your letter of appointment. I confirm that I shall join duty within the stipulated period and would not ask for any extension of the joining period on any account.

I want to assure you once again that I shall spare no pains to prove worthy of the confidence that you have upon me by effecting substantial increase in sales within 2-3 months.

Yours sincerely

Vikram Bahadur Thapa

24. *Letter Declining an Employment*

15 Stamford Road
Singapore

16 April, 19...

The Manager Personnel
Goldstar Enterprises
21, Jalan Besar
Singapore

Dear Sir

Thank you for your letter of 10 April, 19... offering me the post of Asst. Finance Secretary. However, I am sorry to say that now I am unable to accept the position offered. This offer is now quite late and I have already joined another establishment on the same attractive salary and favourable terms and conditions as Asst. Secretary Finance.

I once again thank you for your kind offer, however belated.

I hope you will soon find another suitable candidate for this post.

Yours faithfully

Lak Moy Soon

THIRTEEN

TRAVEL TOURS AND HOTELS

1. *Enquiry about Fares etc.*

Dr. JULIAN MARCOS
12, Rizal Avenue
Manila, (Philippines)

2 April, 19...

The Manager
Indian Airlines
113, Gurudwara Rakabganj Road
New Delhi-110001

Dear Sir

We, a group of seven travellers are interested in visiting places of interest in India interconnected by your Airlines under the "Discover India Fare" scheme.

Please, therefore, send us details relating to fares, flight schedule, baggage allowance, hand-baggage etc. Kindly also inform us about the charges for children below 7 years of age. Further we would like to visit Andaman Islands (Port-Blair) while visiting the southern part of India.

We look forward to your early response and details.

Yours sincerely

Julian Marcos

2. *Letter Requesting Hotel Reservation*

Rex Store Inc.
1257, C.M. Rectro Avenue, Manila
(Philippines)

10 March, 19...

The Manager
RELC International House
30, Orange Course Road
Singapore-1025

Dear Sir

Please reserve and book a suite for our Managing Director Dr. H.G. Gomez, for a week beginning 3rd April to 9th April, 19... He will be accompanied by his personal secretary. The suite should be on the third floor with a spacious balcony overlooking a park or picturesque scenary.

Dr. Gomez will be in the city on business and is expected to check in at about 3 p.m. on 3 April, 19... and check out in the afternoon on 9 April, 19...

Please let us know your confirmation and the rates for the suite and food etc. by 25th March.

Yours faithfully

William Lindsay
Sy. Personal Manager

3. *Letter Enquiring about Hotel Accommodation*

2, Ferry Road
Hongkong

9 October, 19...

The Manager
Hayatt Hotel
28, Jalan Marawan
Jakarta

Dear Sir

One of my friends, who visited Jakarta last year and stayed at your hotel, has recommended it to me. I want to visit your city along with my family in the last week of November .

Would you please send me your rates of two small rooms with toilets attached inclusive of breakfast, lunch and dinner etc.? In all we are four persons: my wife and myself and our two sons aged 7 and 10. We would prefer the rooms adjacent to each other on the third floor with balconies overlooking natural scene.

Favour us with you reply immediately so that we may reserve for rooms at the earliest and make arrangement for our travel to Jakarta.

Yours sincerely

B.C. Drake

4. *Reply to the above*

Hayatt Hotel
28, Jalan Marawan
Jakarta

15 October, 19...

Dear Mr. Drake

Thank you for your letter of 9th October, 19... enquiring about accommodation in our hotel. It was nice of your friend to have recommended our hotel to you and we look forward to offer our service to you and the members of your family.

We shall be glad to provide you two adjacent airconditioned rooms with all the modern facilities in the third floor. The rooms have balconies overlooking picturesque scenery.

We are enclosing a brochure giving details of our rates etc. But you should immediately send your reservation order because the tourist season has just set in and we would not like to disappoint you.

Yours sincerely

Subandrio Ahmed

5. *Another Letter Seeking Hotel Reservation*

12, Corporation Road
Singapore

12 September, 19...

The Manager
Hyatt Regency
Madam Cama Place
R.K. Puram, New Delhi

Dear Sir

I am interested in visiting Delhi in coming October along with my wife. We shall reach Delhi early in the morning of 12 October by Singapore Airlines and drive straight to the hotel. We shall stay in Delhi for a week or ten days.

Ours is purely a personal pleasure trip entailing short trips to Agra and Khajuraho. For our stay there we want one large luxury room on the second floor with T.V., A.C. and phone facilities.

The name of your hotel has been suggested by one of my colleagues who with his family has enjoyed your hospitality.

I should feel obliged if you could confirm the above reservation at the earliest. Let me also know about your room and service charges.

Yours sincerely

Tan Lee Huang

6. *Reply to the above*

Hayatt Regency
Madam Cama Place
R.K. Puram
New Delhi

20 September, 19...

Dear Mr. Huang

Thank you for your letter of 12 September 19... requesting us to reserve for a large luxury room on the second floor with all modern facilities.

We shall keep the desired accommodation reserved for you for 10 days beginning from 12 October, 19...

Please confirm this by return of post or over telephone as this is the tourist season and the bookings are heavy; we would never like you to be disappointed.

Enclosed is a brochure containing details of rooms and service charges. We hope you would give us an opportunity to welcome and serve you and your wife at our hotel.

Yours sincerely

Prem Narain Metha
Manager

7. *Letter to a Travel Agent for Arranging a Business Trip*

Reliance Plastics Sdn. Bhd.
31 B, Medan Imbi
55100 Kuala Lumpur

10 December, 19...

The Manager
ASM Travel Sdn. Bhd.
3, Jalan Tiga, Sungei Besi
Kuala Lumpur

Dear Sir

Our Managing Director Mr. Alean Tan would be on a foreign business trip for 20 days from 15 January to 4 February, 19... He will be on tour to the Middle East countries of Jordan, Iran and Saudi Arabia.

While the exact tour programme of our M.D. is being chalked out, I may inform you tantatively that Mr. Tan would fly from Kuala Lumpur to Iran (Tehran) in the night of 15th Jan. 19... At Tehran he would stay for four days and then leave for Saudi Arabia (Riyadh). There his stay is for a week. On 28th of January he has to attend a conference in Jordan (Amman) in the afternoon. The next day he is scheduled to reach Delhi where he will stay for 2 days. Then he will fly back to Kuala Lumpur.

After reaching Delhi he will take care of his schedule personally. Your responsibility, therefore, is over with Mr. Tan's arrival in India (Delhi).

Meanwhile it would be much appreciated if you could chalk out a flight schedule and forward the same to us for our perusal so that we may immediately order for your personalised services in respect of air-ticketing etc.

We look forward to your immediate response and details.

Yours sincerely

Peter Dickins
Programme Manager

8. *Letter Chartering a Tourist Bus*

International Link Sdn. Bhd.
19, Jalan Ampang
Kuala Lumpur

10 June, 19...

The Manager
Ever on Wheels Tours
Kuala Lumpur

Dear Mr. Abrar Ahmed

This has reference to the visit of our representative Mr. Martin Mathews last week to your office to discuss about chartering of a luxury bus on the permanent basis initially for six months for our business guests and visitors from foreign countries.

Since our business guests and visitors come in batches round the year, it has been decided that we have an A.C. luxury tourist bus with music and video facilities on permanent basis for sight seeing tours on competitive rates.

Besides the fixed monthly payment to you as a renting fee, the actual expenses regarding diesel/petrol consumption, daily charges of drivers, conductors etc. will be paid separately by us. This payment is in addition to the above fixed monthly charges when tours actually take place.

It may be informed to you that the matter has not been finalised yet though we are very much eager to finalise it because one batch of our foreign visitors would soon be here.

Our representative would call on you again in a day or two. We hope you will sign a contract with him in this respect.

Yours sincerely

Nam Tin Tan
Director Tours

9. *Letter about Seminar Facility in a Hotel*

Tractors Singapore Ltd.
26, Banol Sector
Jurongg, Singapore

27 April, 19...

The Manager
New Park Hotel
181, Kitchner Road
Singapore-0820

Dear Sir

Our company has to conduct a seminar for a week from 10th May to 16th May, 19... There would be about 50 participants from Singapore and abroad. For this purpose we want six large luxury rooms for our foreign executive participants and guests and a hall for seminar. The seminar hall should be well equipped with state of the art communication system.

We shall appreciate if you could inform us about your tariff for the above accommodation for a week including the usage of seminar hall, breakfast, lunch, evening tea etc. (but not dinner) for 50 persons.

We expect a package deal on competitive terms as we already have a few good offers from some other hotels of repute in the city, but we could prefer your hotel on account of its convenient location.

We look forward to your immediate response.

Yours sincerely

Robert Teo Keng
Dy. Manager

FOURTEEN

RAIL, ROAD AND SEA TRANSPORT

1. *Complaint to the Railway Authorities*

Samtex Enterprise
1231, Jalan, 11 Ampang
New Village
Kuala Lumpur

19 April, 19...

The General Manager
Malayan Railway Adminstration
Kuala Lumpur

Dear Sir

We despatched a parcel by passenger train on 10th April, 19... against your Railway recept no. 22713 of the same date.

The parcel was addressed to Pro-Tech Sdn. Bhd., Johor Bahru. It is now more than 8 days back that we sent this parcel. The consignees have informed us today on telephone that the parcel has not reached them so far. We wonder whether the parcel has been miscarried.

We, therefore, request you to make immediate enquiries into the matter and let us have a prompt reply. We are really anxious as the parcel contains perishable items and were urgently needed by the consignees.

We look forward to your immediate reply and action.

Yours faithfully,

Suthon Suchinta,
Manager.

Encl : Photocopy of the R/R No. 22713

2. *Notifying Despatch of Goods by Railway Parcel*

MEDICHEM SYSTEMS SDN BHD
5 Lrg. Perusahann 3 B. Caves
Kuala Lumpur

Telephone : 03-688 8611

4 March, 19...

The Manager
Uttama Clinic Sdn. Bhd.
Kota Baharu

Dear Sir

We thank you for your order no. 4721 of 25th February, 19... for drugs and medicines worth $ 500. We have despatched these today by railway parcel as requested. We hope the medicines would reach you within 3-4 days.

We are drawing the amount of $ 500 by V.P.P. and in the V.P.P. cover we have enclosed the Railway receipt no. 3210 dated 04/03/19... to enable you to clear the parcel of medicine.

We hope you will find this consignment of medicine in goods condition and look forward for a repeat order.

Yours sincerely

Mubarak Hussain

3. *Letter to Railway Authorities Requesting Redirection of Consignment*

Libra Industries Pvt. Ltd.
Jalan Tukang
Singapore

7 July, 19...

The Manager
Railway Administration
Keppel Road, Singapore

Dear Sir

We sent a Railway parcel to Unic Enterprises, Petaling Jaya, Selangor on 30 June, 19... against Railway receipt no. 7271. The R/R and invoices relating to this parcel were sent by us to the above firm by V.P.P. as requested by them, but surprisingly enough they have failed to honour the V.P.P.

Since they have failed to honour the above V.P.P., we request you to redirect this Railway parcel to our address in Kuala Lumpur. We are enclosing a copy of the R/R and shall pay all the charges on the delivery of the parcel.

Yours faithfully

Wong Shee Fun

4. *Enquiry about Freight and Sailing Schedule*

FEDERAL TELE COMMUNICATIONS SDN BHD
7, Jalan Manis Empat, Taman Segar
Kuala Lumpur

Telephone : 03-7560211

20 January, 19...

The Manager
Malaysia Shipping Corpn. Sdn. Bhd.
Compleks Nagaria, Kulala Lumpur

Dear Sir

We want to despatch 10 cases of communication items measuring 1x1 1/2 m. each weighing 100 kgs. next month to Colombo (Sri Lanka) by sea.

Therefore, we would appreciate your quotation for freight for above shipment. Further intimate us your sailing schedule and the time taken in the voyage from Kuala Lumpur to Colombo.

You will have to collect the consignment from our above address and then lead it into your cargo liner at the port.

We look forward to your early response.

Yours faithfully

Theo Choo Gan

5. *Asking the Agent to Collect Consignment for Shipping*

ALL MALAYA TEXTILE SDN BHD
16, Jalan Pudu, Kuala Lumpur

2 April, 19...

The Manager
Dora Express Sdn. Bhd.
Menara Maybank
Kuala Lumpur

Dear Sir

Further to our telephonic talk with you day before yesterday, we want to inform you that 5 bales of clothes are ready for despatch to Jakarta by sea to our clients:

Aman Traders
291 Jalan Sultan
Jakarta
(Indonesia)

Relevant shipping documents including invoices, account for transport charges are also ready.

Therefore, you are requested to do the needful immediately under advice to us.

Yours faithfully

Martin Gay
Manager

6. Agents Reply to the above

Dora Express Sdn. Bhd.
Menra Maybank
Kuala Lumpur

4 April, 19...

The Manager
All Malaya Textile Sdn. Bhd.
16, Jalan Pudu
Kuala Lumpur

Dear Mr. Martin Gay

We thank you for informing us that 5 bales of clothes along with their shipping documents are now ready for collection and loading.

Now, please arrange to send the bales by a road transport carrier to Port Kelang to be shipped to Jakarta in our cargo liner. The cargo can be loaded at dock number 7 within this week before the departure date. Also send the duly filled in and signed contract and shipping form.

Yours faithfully

Noor Mohmod
Manager

7. *Letter Asking Freight Rates from a Transport Operator*

THE COASTAL CHEMICALS SDN BHD
No. 98, Jalan Dato Haji Eusoff, Kuala Lampur

Telefax : 03-441 4244

15 July, 19...

The Manager
Lanfong Trading & Transport Company
12, Jalan Merimau, Kuala Lampur
(Malaysia)

Dear Sir

Our company the Coastal Chemicals Sdn. Bhd. produces industrial explosives and chemicals. We export these items to various foreign countries, particularly to the Middle East and Australia in bulk almost every month. We require the services of 2-3 containers to transport these items in to port Kelang for our warehouse at Jalan Ipoh.

As these items are mainly chemicals and industrial explosives, they need to be handled and transported very carefully in well secured large container-trailers meant for bonded cargoes.

We require your container services within last week of every month. We shall inform you about the actual date and time of transportation 24 hours before the scheduled time.

We would appreciate if you send us your quotation for the container service on the competitive basis initially for the period of 6 months beginning from the next month. This contract may be renewed for a longer period subject to our full satisfaction.

We look forward to your early quotation so that the matter may be processed and finalised soon.

Yours faithfully

Karimuddin
Manager

8. *Letter Asking Quotation for Transportation of Office Equipment etc.*

MODERN COOLING TOWERS SDN BHD
Jalan Amborg Dua (Jln 4), Kepong Baru
Kuala Lumpur (Malaysia)

Telephone : 03-621 0289
Fax : 03-621 0289

10 August, 19...

The Manager
New Nam Pong Transport Company
12, Large Brunet
Kuala Lampur

Dear Mr. Lian Soon

We are shifting some our office equipment, furniture etc. from the above office to our new Branch Office at 40G, Jalan Lima, Jalan Chan Sow Lin, Kuala Lumpur and want to commence functioning from there next Monday the 16th August.

Therefore we would like you to quote your transportation charges for carrying our office equipment etc. containing computers, almirahs, tables, chairs, typewriters, airconditioners, fax machine, boxes of stationery, office records etc.

For the above purpose we would like that your representative calls on us at an early date to asses the load and volume of items to be transported to our new branch office. We would prefer to shift either in the early morning or late in the evening when there is not much rush of traffic. You may please contact me on the telephone to fix an appointment with me.

Yours sincerely

Ronger Koo
Manager

9. *A Circular from Transporters*

COMMONWEALTH TRANSPORT SERVICES PTE LTD
New Bridge Road, Chaina Point, Singapore

Telephone : 532 2466
Fax : 532 4631

5 January, 19...

Dear Sir/Madam

We take this opportunity to introduce ourselves as road carriers and transporters. We are well-known for prompt service throughout the country.

We undertake transportation of all kinds of general, bonded project, and heavy cargoes from Singapore to any part of the state and to Kuala Lumpur and all other destination of Malaysia. We have regular service to and from some of these cities.

Our large fleet contains trailers, a hydraulic trailer, trucks and lorries. We also undertake sea and air forwarding and customs clearance service. As we have a couple of associate transport companies, we can move and transport your goods and merchandise very fast and quickly. Our rates are competitive and our services punctual, reliable, safe and prompt.

We are enclosing a brochure to give you more details about our services and look forward to an early opportunity to serve you.

Yours faithfully

Geore Lim
Manager

FIFTEEN

COMMERCIAL TERMINOLOGY

There are many words and phrases of specific kind used in business correspondence. These terms are very useful as they are in common use in business correspondence and transactions. The thorough knowledge of these is of vital importance for one who wants to be efficient and skilled in writing business letters. Here below is a comprehensive list of such commercial and business terms and phrases for your benefit.

Abandonment : The surrender of giving up of rights, interest or property in favour of another person expressly or by implication.

Acceptance : A terms applied to a bill of exchange after it has been honoured by the drawee. Writing of name across the face of the bill constitutes acceptance.

Account : In accounting it means a ledger sheet showing debits and credits of any asset, liability etc. In business it means details regarding goods supplied to a customer.

Account Current : Statement of accounts showing the daily balance and adding or deducting interest there on.

Account Payable : A debt, owing to an enterprise which arises in the normal course of business dealing and is not supported by negotiable paper.

Accrue : To accumulate as interest.

Acknowledgement : Verification of a letter of order received.

Advance : Money paid before it is due.

Advance Bill : A bill of exchange drawn before shipment of goods.

Advice : Information sent by one businessman to another specially in connection with the forwarding of goods.

Ad valorem : According to value.

After Right : Payment of bills days after presentation.

Affidavit : A written oath.

After date : Payment of bill or invoices after the date specified in the documents.

Agent : A person who acts for another.

Agreements : A written or an oral contract to do or not to do certain things.

Amortization : The gradual payment of a debt at regular intervals.

Anti-date : A date written on a document prior to that on which it was drawn.

Annuity : The investment that produces fixed yearly payments.

Allonge : A slip of paper pasted on Bill of Exchange of continuation of endorsements.

All Risk Insurance (a.a.r.) : Against all risks. An insurance policy insuring against loss caused by all perils except those specially mentioned in the policy.

Appeal Bond : A bond required of an appellant to assure payment of costs and damages if the appeal is lost.

Appraise : To evaluate.

Appraiser : One empowered to evaluate property of all kinds.

Appreciate : To increase in value.

Assess : To evaluate for the purpose of taxation etc.

Assets : The stock in trade of a business. All property that may be pledged against advances or loans.

Article of Association : The document in which are defined the powers, rights, duties, authority and liablities of the shareholders and directors of a limited company. It is a set of rules for the internal management of the company.

Amalgamate : Join together two or more companies etc.

Adjustments : Changes and alterations.

Approval (on) : To send goods for inspection with a choice to return if not required.

Arrears : Overdue debts.

Arbitration : Setting disputes by some one chosen to hear both sides and come to a decision.

At maturity : On becoming due.

Audit : Checking a business's financial records.

Bearer : The possessor of document.

Bid : Statement of the price.

Bill of Exchange : An order drawn by one person on another in favour of a third for the payment of the sum of money mentioned therein within a fixed time.

Bill of Landing : A document issued by the carrier to the shipper as a receipt and as a contract governing transportation and delivery of the articles only.

Back Bill : A statement of unpaid charges

Bad debt : A debt which is no more expected to be recovered.

Balance : The excess amount in an account.

Balance Sheet : A statement showing the assets and liabilities of an organisation or company.

Bank Acceptance : A bill of exchange accepted by a bank for payment.

Bankruptcy : A state of insolvency when the effects of a man unable to pay his debts are taken over by a trustee and distributed for the benefit of all the creditors.

Bill of Entry : A document describing goods before they are landed, which importers give to customs authorities.

Beneficiary : A person to receive benefit from will etc.

Boom : To advertise on vast scale.

Bond : A sealed document by which a person binds himself, his heirs, executors and administrators to pay a certain sum to another person on or before a specified date.

Bonded Goods : Goods stored in a warehouse by an owner who has furnished a bond to pay duty of taxes due.

Bonded Store : A place where goods are stored for the purpose of customs duty.

Bonded Warehouse : A government building in which bonded goods are stored.

Brand : Trade mark used on marketable goods.

By Separate Post : Separately, by another post.

Brochure : A pamphlet, a small hand book.

Breach of Contract : Violation of a contract by non- performance of doing some such act contrary to the terms and conditions of the contract.

Broker : An agent who buys and sells an behalf of others without taking possession of the goods.

Brokerage : The commission paid to the agent as his remuneration.

Bursar : Treasurer, especially of an educational institution.

Bulk Cargoes : Goods not packed but loaded loose.

Capital : The sum of money invested in a business.

Carriage : Transportation of goods.

Carriage Paid : The transport-expenses paid by the seller.

Carriage Forward : The buyer pays the delivery charges.

Cash : Money in hand: To buy for cash means to buy for immediate payment.

Cash Against Documents : Payment made on delivery of shipping documents.

Cash-book : A book in which cash transactions are recorded.

Cash Discount : Discount allowed for payment of debt in advance.

Caveat Emptor : Let the buyer beware, one buys at his own risk.

Caveat Venditor : Let the seller beware. It is antonym of caveat emptor.

Charter Party : A document which sets forth the agreement between parties hiring a ship for a voyage or a period.

Certificate of Origin : A document entitling importer to preferential customers duties.

Cheque : It is a bill of exchange drawn on a banker and payable on demand.

(1) *Bearer cheque* — A cheque that is payable to payee or bearer.

(2) *Order cheque* — A cheque payable to payee on order.

(3) *Crossed cheque* — A cheque payable to the payee's account only.

(4) *Post-dated cheque* — A cheque bearing a future date.

(5) *State cheque* — A cheque which has not been presented with the stipulated period.

Cif Value : Value covering cost, insurance and freight.

Circular Note : A letter of credit issued by a bank to client enabling the holders to obtain payment at various places abroad.

Client : A customer.

Clientele : Clients or patrons as a group.

Closing Price : The price at which the last sales of an organised market is made on a particular date.

Commission : The remuneration paid to an agent for his services.

Common Carrier : An authorised transport agency which requires the carrier to serve all the people.

Collateral : Property used as security for a loan.

Compensation : Money paid to make good the loss.

Common Law : Usages and customs, which have sanctioned precedents, but are not reduced to codes.

Company : As association of persons formed for purpose of profit and contributing to a common capital.

Concern : A firm or business establishment.

Confirm : A verbal agreement or order put into black and white.

Consignee : The person to whom goods are sent.

Consigner : The one who sends the goods.

Consignment : The goods sent to another person for sale.

Contract : A legal agreement between two or more persons supported by consideration.

Counter Sign : To authenticate by putting additional signature.

Cover : Money deposited as security against possible loss.

Cover Note : A document issued by insures giving temporary insurance cover pending the issue of formal insurance policy.

Credential : A certificate showing one's authority or claim.

Credit : Ability to secure goods or services in the present against the promise to pay later.

Credit Letter : A letter given to a representative going abroad instructing a banker to meet the drafts against that letter up to a specified limit.

Commitments : Carrying out of certain duties on promise.

Courier : A travelling attendent.

Current Demand : Demand of product at the present time.

Covering letter : A letter with which certain documents are enclosed.

Counter Offer : An alternative offer to that of another man.

Clearing Agents : Agents who clear goods from ships, rail, transport companies etc.

Consultant : One who advises in a profession.

Credit worthy : Believed to be financially sound.

Credit Standing : Financial reputation.

Cut losses : Reduce losses.

Comply with : To carry out.

Commission House : A commission agency.

Conviction : A strong belief.

Consular Invoice : An invoice signed by the Embassy of a country before it is sent to that country.

Covenant : A clause in a deed.

Currently : At the present time.

Custom : Duty assessed by law.

Creditor : One whom debt in owned.

Current Account : A business account with a bank for collecting and paying accounts.

Curriculum vitae : A brief account of one's previous career, resume.

Date of Maturity : Date on which a debt becomes due for payment.

Days of Grace : Extra time allowed for making certain payments.

Dead Stock : Inventory for which there is little or no demand.

Dead Weight : The weight of freight carrying vehicles without load.

Debenture : A document issued under the seal of the company, usually charging all or some of the company's property. The rate of interest payable, the time of redemption are clearly mentioned in it.

Debit : An amount owing to another person.

Debit Note : If the supplier has under-charged, a debit note may be sent to the buyer.

Debtor : A person, firm or company which owes a certain amount of money.

Default : Failure to perform a term of contract at the stipulated time.

Defer Payment : Pay at a later date.

Deferred Rebate : Discount to be allowed later.

Deficit : A money shortage.

Demurrage : Money paid for any delay in getting goods unloaded beyond a specified date.

Deposit : Money placed with another for safe custody.

Depreciation : Reduction in value.

Disclaim : Refuse to be responsible.

Demonstrate : To show how a thing works.

Discount : A reduction in price.

Dishonour : Refuse to pay a cheque etc.

Display : To arrange goods is a window or a counter for sale.

Deadline : The final date of payment

Drawer : A person who draws a bill etc.

Draw : To fill up a cheque, bill etc.

Drawee : The persoh who will have to pay the bill etc.

Draw on us : Send a bill of exchange for our acceptance.

Draft : Bill of exchange.

Duplicate : Two copies.

Devaluation : Reduction in value of a currency at time when goods are in the factory or warehouse.

Dividend : The income on investment. Profits of a company distributed among shareholders.

Dry-goods : Textile fabrics.

Endorse : To sign the payee's name on the back of a cheque etc.

Endorsement : The act of enclosing.

Endorser : The payee.

Endowment : Money given.

Entry : The written of a transaction.

Estimate : A valuation, a statement of terms.

Excise Duty : Taxes levied by the government on article manufactured for consumption.

Exemption : Money not subject to taxation.

Extension : Extra time allowed for making a payment.

Executor : A person appointed by a will to see that its provisions are carried out.

Expressed Warranty : A statement of conduct by a seller to a buyer that a specific condition exists in the charter of goods.

Ex Ship : The quoted price includes delivery over the side of the ship.

External Debt : The debt held by persons outside the country.

Ex-godown : The buyer is responsible for goods once they leave the godown.

Firm Order : A definite order.

Fascimile : An exact copy.

Firm Condition : A condition that must be adhered to.

Forfeiture : Loss of money as a penalty for default.

Freightage : Transportation charges for goods. The goods so carried.

Free on board (f.o.b.) : The quotation covers the cost of loading the goods on the ship, after that the buyer becomes responsible for all charges.

Forwarding Agents : Agents who arrange for transportation of goods.

Face Value : The value stated on the face of a security.

Free on Rail (f.o.r.) : The quotation covers the cost of loading the goods on rail.

Goodwill : Value of a firm's reputation.

Gilt-edged Securities : Stock on which interest is not only safe but also sufficiently high.

Grace Period : Period granted to a debtor by a creditor beyond due date.

Gross Profit : Total allocated receipts of a period's operations less the cost of goods sold, before allowing for operating expenses and income tax.

Gross Proceeds : Proceeds before deductions of expenses.

Gross Weight : Total weight.

Guarantor : A person who agrees to be responsible for another person's debt.

Handbill : Small poster advertising goods etc.

Hardware : Manufactured metal articles.

Hire Purchase : A system for the purchase of goods or property by which they are obtained on hire and each payment is also treated as a part payment of the purchase.

Hold-ups : Delays.

Hypothecation : Pledging of goods, securities etc.

Honour of Cheque : To accept and pay for a cheque.

Imports : Goods brought from foreign countries

Indemnity : Security against loss and damage.

Indent : An order for goods. It also means a requisition for stores.

Identical : Exactly similar.

Instalments : Partial payments made at stated intervals.

Intransit : During transportation.

In Full Settlement : In full payment of one's debts

Initial Advertising : Advertising in the earlier stages.

Irrevocable : That which cannot be changed or cancelled.

Instruments : A legal drawn up formal document.

Insure : Protect from loss and damage.

Immaterial : Of not much significance

Inland Bill : A bill of exchange drawn and payable within the country.

Inscribed Stock : Company or Government stock for which no certificates are issued.

Insolvent : One unable to pay debts.

Inter-alia : Among other things.

Interest : An amount paid on loan or debt.

(1) *Simple Interest* — This is paid only on sum lent.

(2) *Compound Interest* — This is paid on sum lent and the accumulated unpaid interest.

Interim Bond : A temporary certificate which is replaced by a permanent bond later.

Invalid Note : When a promissory note is obtained by misrepresentation or under threat or for illegal gratification the note becomes invalid.

Inventory : An itemized list of merchandise or property.

Invoice : A written statement of goods purchased or sold showing particulars of prices, discounts etc.

Item : A separate entry in an account.

I.O.U. : I owe you, an acknowledgement of debt.

Jerquer : A customs official who searches ships for dutiable articles. He also checks ship's papers relating to import of goods.

Jettison : The throwing overboard a ship goods etc. on account of bad weather or enemy action etc. The owner of the property sacrified for the preservation of the whole, has a claim upon the owners of the property preserved, who are bound to share his loss with him.

Jury : A bench of persons chosen and sworn to hear and pass verdict upon evidence brought forward in a trial in quest of or inquiry.

Lag Behind : To follow slowly.

Layout : Arrangement of a letter or advertisement

Lease : To rent or let.

Legal Tender : Paper or metal money that a Government decrease must be accepted as a lawful payment for debts and purchases.

Letter of Allotment : A letter informing an applicant for shares etc. that certain shares etc. been allotted to him or her.

Letter of Credit : A letter written by a person to another directing him to pay or hold a certain sum of money at the disposal of the third party. It is not transferable by endorsement.

Letterhead : Heading printed at the top of a sheet of letter paper.

Liabilities : Debts etc.

Liable : A statement damaging a person's reputation.

License : Permission given to do some act etc. without which it would be unlawful.

Lien : A legal right of a person to detain or control property belonging to another until certain charges upon it have been paid or until some pecuniary claim against the owner has been satisfied.

Liquidation : The winding up affairs of an organisation.

Liquidity : Ability to turn assets into cash.

List Price : The price shown in the sales list of the seller.

Long Bills : Bill of exchange drawn payable at period exceeding three days after date of sight.

Manifest : A list of goods on board of a ship.

Margin : A percentage deposited with a broker to secure him against loss by violent fluctuation of price.

Maritime : Relating to sea.

Marked Cheque : It is a cheque marked by the drawee banker guaranteeing for its being good for payment.

Market Area : That territory within which the products purchase or sale affect the price generally prevailing for that commodity.

Market Price : The price at which the goods are exchanged in market from day-to-day or the current ruling price in the market.

Market Value : The price at which stock, bonds, notes or goods sell in a given market at a given time.

Maturity Date : The date on which an obligation is due.

Maturity Value : The amount which must be paid on the date an obligation is due.

Memorandum of Association : It is a document which indicates the name, address, objects and powers, the limitation of members, liability, and the share capital of the company. It further defines the limits of fields of operations.

Merchandise : Goods, items of commerce.

Merger : Combination of one or more companies into one

Middleman : One who stands in between producer or manufacturer and the consumer.

Monetary : Relating to money.

Monopoly : Market situation in which one person of a group has such a control of the supply of a commodity as to be able to regulate its price.

Mortgage : A deed transferring property to a creditor as security for the payment of debt.

Negotiate : To conduct business transactions. To pass a cheque. To discount a bill of exchange.

Negotiable Instruments : Such as bills, notes, cheques, bonds and other documents which by common usage on transfer by delivery from one person to another, convey a right to the property therein free from all claims.

Net : The remainder after all deductions.

Net Profit : Profit after all deductions.

Net Sales : The total of all sales after deduction returned sales.

Networking : The establishing of business and professional contacts.

Nominal Small : Nominal fee.

Normal Price : The price which will in the long run make the rate of production and rate of consumption equal.

Notary : A person duly authorised by Government to take oaths, attest writings etc.

Notorial Protest : That evidence required by law of the due presentation of a bill for acceptance or payment.

Obligation : Any enforceable debt (business). A duty owed by one person to another (Legal).

Obsolete : That which is no longer in use.

Octroi : A tax imposed on articles coming inside a city. Revenue from such source generally go to municipal bodies.

Official Exchange Rate : The ratio which is applied by the monetary authority of one country in exchange for that of another country.

On Account : As in part payment

On approval : To send goods for inspection with discretion to return if not required.

Open Cheque : An uncrossed cheque payable on presentation to bearer to order as the case may be.

Open Credit : Credit given by a banker to customer without guarantee or security.

Open Indent : An importer's purchase order to an exporter, which may be filed with goods from any manufacturer or firm provided the goods meet specification.

Opening Price : The price at which the first sale in an organised market is made on a particular day.

Open Letter of Credit : A letter of credit with special conditions.

Open Rate : The market rate.

Oral Notification : A verbal message.

Options : The right to act on an offer at a fixed price within a limited time.

Order : Verbal or written instruction for the purchase of goods.

Output : The quantity of goods produced in a given time.

Over Draft : A draft drawn in excess of the amount owed by the party upon whom the draft is drawn.

Over Drawn : Withdrawn in excess of balance available.

Outstanding Balance : Amount still owing.

Par : A stock or bond selling for exactly the amount expressed upon its face is said to be at par. When selling at a profit it is said to be "Above Par". When selling at a loss, it is called "Below Par".

Par of Exchange : The value of a country's money in that of the other, comparing gold with gold and silver with silver.

Par Value : In the case of bonds and stocks, the face value appearing on the certificate is the par value.

Passing Phase : A temporary state of affairs. The dullness in wool trade is a passing phase.

Patents : A patent is an exclusive right granted under the Patents Act to the inventor of a new useful technical invention.

Patent Infringement : Unauthorised use, sale or manufacture of a patened article.

Payee : The person named on a cheque, bill of exchange or other document who is to receive payment.

Pay In : The money deposited in a bank.

Payment of Invoice : Payment becomes due as soon as the invoice is presented.

Payment on Account : Part payment

Periodical : Issued at regular intervals.

Personnel : Employees, staff.

Petty Cash : A cash or fund for small disbursements. It is also termed as petty fund.

Pilferages : Small thefts.

Plaitiff : One who brings a suit in a court of law.

Pledge : It is a bailment of personal property by the owner to another as security for a debt.

Policy : In insurance, it is the contract between the insurer and the insured setting forth the various terms and conditions of the contract.

Pool : A combination formed to control the price of merchandise.

Portfolio : The various securities held by an investor

Post Dated : It is said of a cheque or other document which bears a date subsequent to the date of delivery.

Power of Attorney : A document authorizing a person to act legally for another.

Preliminary Negotiation : Earlier discussion regarding terms.

Prepaying : Paying before the date on which payment is due.

Prospective : Possible, likely, expected-prospective customers.

Push your Products : Make extra efforts in selling goods.

Post (By Separate) : By another post.

Pending : Unsettled.

Prestige : Reputation.

Productivity : Rate of yield or output.

Proforma : Latin for "for the sake of form". Used to describe in accounting, financial and other statements of conclusions based upon assumed or anticipated facts.

Proforma Invoiced : An invoice sent for the information of buyer.

Premium : Payment for insurance.

Proposal Form : A written application for covering insurance.

Price : The amount of money which expresses exchange value of a single unit of goods, as 1000 grams, or 1 kilo of tea leaves.

Promissory Note : A written promise by a person to pay a specified amount on a specified date

Property : Premises

Prorata : In proportion to respective right or liabilities.

Proprietor : Owner

Prospectus : Circular containing an outline of an article: commercial enterprise for public favour comment.

Provision : A term or condition in an agreement.

Proviso : Conditional stipulation.

Proxy : Authorised to vote for shareholder at a meeting

Quantity discount : A discount allowed on the principle that large quantity involve lower costs.

Quorum : The minimum number of persons required to be present at a meeting.

Quotation : The current published price of any commodity or security. Often two prices are given: (1) the price asked for sellers; (2) the price offered by buyers.

Rate : The charge per unit for goods or services.

Range (a big) : A wide variety.

Rate war : Cut throat competition between two or more carriers in an effort to attract freight by cutting rates.

Rejected : Refused-Goods will be rejected if they do not tally the sample.

Resources : Financial means.

Reputable : Having good reputation.

Revocable : Which can be changed or cancelled.

Representative : An agent or a salesman.

Return : The full account of business transaction.

Returns : The proceeds of a business transactions.

Security : Bonds, shares or other property pledged to cover a debt.

Sabotage : Deliberate conduct damaging machinery, destroying raw materials, or turning out defective work.

Shareholder or *Stockholders* : The owner of a stock certificate. A part owner of the corporation.

Shipment : Article put on board the ship for transportation.

Sight : Said of bills of exchange payable when received and in which no days of grace are allowed.

Sight Bill : A bill payable on sight as soon as it is presented.

Sight Draft : A cheque or draft on bank, commercial house, or debtor which demands payment immediately upon presentation.

Software : The date and programming of a computer

Sixty(60) Days, Sight : For payment within 60 days of acceptance.

Sleeping Partnership : One in which only capital is furnished and no active part is taken in business.

Slump : A period of bad trade caused by lack of demand of commodities.

Solvency : The ability to discharge all debts and obligations in full.

Special Agent : An agent whose powers to act for his principal are limited.

Special Concessions : More discounts.

Settlement : Settlement of Bills.

Statement of Account : Statement showing debit or credit balance of a client.

Substitute : Alternative.

Sole-Agent : The only agent.

Standing : Established reputation.

Specification : Of full details about material used.

Solicited : Asked for.

Sole Charges : Full charge.

Substantial : Considerable in amount.

Speciality : An article dealt in chiefly or exclusively.

Spot price : The price for goods deliverable immediately.

Speculation : Selling of goods or securities in the hope of making a profit from the change in price.

Standing Order : An order to make certain payments at stated times.

Syndicate : A combination of persons or firms to achieve a common business purpose.

Trade Reference : Name of persons (traders) to whom a reference may be made.

Tabulated : Presented in the form of a table - A tabulated quotation.

Tariff : In protection for indigenous industry or measures undertaken by any country to protect its own industry against trade competition from outside.

Tax : A compulsory payment of the Government to defray the expense which it has incurred in performing services for the common benefit.

Testimonial : Certificate.

Trend : General tendency.

Triplicate : Three copies - Please send your bill in triplicate.

Turn Over : Total sales - The total turn over of the firm is five crores.

Tender : 'An offer to buy or sell.

Terms : Conditions on which an agreement is made or on which a sale is made.

Time Bill : A bill of exchange payable at a future date rather than immediately.

Trade Bill : A bill of exchange drawn by the seller of the goods on the buyer covering payment of the goods.

Trade Discounts : These are the discounts allowed to the middle men.

Trade Mark : A distinctive device or imprint used by a person or firm to identify his products.

Ultimately : Finally.

Undertaking : A promise.

Unqualified Acceptance : Accepting a bill in full.

Unsolicated : Unasked for.

Ultra Vires : Latin word for "beyond the powers". Generally used to describe an act by a corporation or its agent which is beyond the powers to set out in the articles in incorporation.

Underwriter : Any person, banker or syndicate that guarantees to furnish a definite sum of money by a definite date to a business or Government in return for an issue of bonds or stock.

Unilateral Contract : It is a contract that is binding on any one party to it.

Unsecured Creditor : A lender whose loan or debt is not secured by any collateral or mortgage.

Unship : Unload from a ship.

Usance : The customary number of days or months in which foreign bills of exchange are drawn in a certain place.

Vendor : Pedlar or hawker.

Venture : Business enterprise especially of a speculative nature.

Valid : That which holds good—Valid for one month.

Vital : Essential.

Warrant : A magistrate's order for the arrest of a person or seizure of goods; or a receipt for goods deposited in a warehouse, and a negotiable document entitling the holder to certain money or property.

Wash : A fictitious sale or transaction.

Waiver : Forego—Waive clause 7 of the agreement.

Will : Legal disposition of property on one's death according to the written instruction of the deceased.

Without Notice : No previous notice required.

Working Capital : The capital required to keep business running.

Write : A written command in the name of State of Court directing the State or Court to act or abstain from acting in some way.

SIXTEEN

COMMERCIAL ABBREVIATIONS

As far as possible the use of abbreviation should be avoided, unless they are very familiar and common. There is minimum possibility of making mistakes or confusion if words are spelled out in full. However, certain abbreviations are still in common use. A list of some important abbreviations is given below :

A

A1	First class
a.	at the rate of
a.a.r.	against all risks
abbr.	abbreviation
abbrev.	abbreviation
abr.	abridged
abs.	absent
abstr.	abstract
a/c.	account
ac.	account
acct.	account
A/C.	account
A/C.	Account Current
A.D.	Acknowledgement due
a.d.	after date
Advt.	Advertisement
Advert.	Advertisement
Aftn.	afternoon
agcy.	agency
agt.	agent
alt.	alternate
alt.	altitude
alt.	alto

A.M.	ante meridiem (morning-before noon)
amt.	amount
a/o.	account of
appro.	approval
Ad.lib.	Ad libitum (at pleasure)
ad val	ad valorem (according to value)
admin.	administration
ad.	advertisement
advt.	advertisement
aux.	auxiliary
arth	arithmetic
art.	article
A/s	account sales or sales account
assn.	association
assoc.	association
asst.	assistant
asst.	assorted
Aug.	August
Ave.	Avenue

B

bal.	balance
b/d	bill or bank book
bd	board
bd.	bond
bd.	bundle
B.C.	Before Christ
B/E	Bill of Exchnge
bdl	bundle
Bdth.	breadth
b.f.	brough forward
bk.	bank
bk.	book
bk.	book-keeping
B/L	Bill of Lading
b/l	bill of lading
bl.	bale
bl.	barrel
bldg.	building
blk.	bulk
blk.	blank
bot.	bottle
BP.	Bills Payable
bp.	bill of parcel
bp.	boiling point
b.p.	below proof
B.R.	Bills Receivable
B/R	Bills Receivable
Br.	Brother, Branch
brl.	barrel
bro.	brother

bros.	brothers
B.S.	Bill of Sale
B/s	Bill of sale
bs.	balance sheet
b.	bought
bght.	bought
bu.	bushel(s)
bu.	bureau
bu.	bureau
bx.	box

C

C.A.	Chartered Accountant/Cost Accountant
ca.	circa (about)
cap.	capital
cap.	capitalize
capt.	captain
chg.	charge
c.c.	centigrade
cc.	carbon copy
c.c.	cubic centimetre (s)
cent.	centigrade
cent.	centimetre
c.l.	carload
cml.	commercial
Co.	Company
co.	company
co.	company
c.o.	care of
C.O.D.	Cash on Delivery
c.o.d.	cash on delivery
C.E.	Civil Engineer
Col.	Colonel, column
comp.	compound
commn.	commission, communication
comp.	compound
consgt.	consignment
contd.	continued
contr.	contract
Co.Op.	Co-operative Society
Corpn.	Corporation
cent.	a hundred
cf.	refer
cge.pd.	carriage paid
C.H.	Custom House
chem.	chemical
chged.	charged
chm.	chemical
chron.	chronological
Cie.	campaigne
c.i.f.	cost, insurance and freight

C/L	Carload
corr.	correspondence
c.p.	candle power
Cp.	Compare
cpd.	compound
Cr.	Creditor
cr.	credit
C/R	Company's Risk
C/s	cases
ct.	carat
cu.	cubic
cum.div.	with dividend
currt.	current
current	present month of year
C.W.O.	cash with order
Cwt.	hundred weight

D

D.	In Roman numerals 500
d.	date
d/a	documents against acceptance
d/d	delivered
Dec.	December
deg.	degree(s)
del.	deliver
del.	delegate
dely.	delivery
dept.	department
disc.	discount
disct.	discount
Ditto.	the same
d/s	days after sight
dup.	duplicate
div.	dividend
div.	division
divd.	dividend
dk.	dock
dk.	dark
dks.	docks
D/n.	Debit note
do.	ditoo (the same)
D/o	delivery order
dols.	dollars
doz.	dozen
doz.	dozen
d/p	documents against payment
dr.	debtor
Dr.	Debtor/Doctor
dr.	dram
dr.	drawer
d.s.	days after sight
d/y	delivery
dz.	dozen

E

ea.	each
ed.	edited
ed.	edition
ed.	editor
E.E.	Errors Excepted
e.g.	exempli gratia (for example)
encl.	enclosure
E.&.O.E.	errors and omissions excepted
e.o.m.	end of month
etc.	etcetra (and so forth) (and the rest)
et.Cie.	& Compaigne
et,seq.	et sequence (and the following)
ex.	ex godown (form godown)
ex.	example
ex.	exchange
ex.	ex-coupon
exc.	exchange
eq.	equal
esq.	esquire
est.	estimate
est.	established
et. al.	et alibi (and elsewhere)
excl.	exclusive
exec.	executive
ext.	extension
exc.div.	ex.divided (without dividend)

F

F.	Friday
f.a.a.	free of all average
fac.	facsimile
facs.	facsimile
fah.	fahrenheit
fa.q.	fair average quality
f.a.s.	free alongside ship
f.b.	free docks (goods to be delivered)
Feb.	February
fec.	fecit
fig.	figure
f.o.	folio
f.o.b.	free on board
F.O.B.	Free on Board
fol.	folio
folg.	following
F.O.R.	Free on Rail

f.p.	foot pound
f.p.a.	free particulars average (marine insurance)
fr.	Franc
Free case	no charge for case
Fri.	Friday

G

gal.	gallon
gall.	gallon
g.c.f.	greatest common factor
gds.	goods
gn.	general
gm.	gramme
gns.	guineas
gns.	guineas
Gr.	Grains
Gr.	Gross
gr.wt.	gross weight
grs.	gross
g.t.c.	goods till cancelled
guar.	guaranteed
g.v.	grande votesse (Fact goods train)

H

hhd.	hogshead
Hon.	Honourable
hon.	honorary
H.P.	Horse Power
H.P.	Hire Purchase
h.p.	horse power
h.p.n.	horse power nominal
hr.	hour
hrs.	hours
ht.	heat
ht.	height

I

ib.	ibidem (in the same place)
ibid.	ibidem (in the same place)
i.c.	in charge
id.	idem (the same)
i.e.	idest (that is)
I.H.P.	indicated horse power
imp.	important
imp.	imported
in.	inch

inc.	incorporated
Inc.	Incorporated
inc.	including
inc.	incomplete
Incorp.	Incorporated
in ex.	in extenso
inf.	information
inf.	infra (below)
ins.	insurance
inst.	instant (present month)
int.	interest
inv.	invoice
I/O	inspecting order
I.O.U.	I owe you
ital	italics

J

Jan.	January
Jr.	Junior
Jul	July
Jun.	June

K

k.	kilo
k.g.	kilogram
kild.	kilderkin
klo.	kilo
klo.	kilo
km.	kilometre
k.o.	killo
kt.	carat
kw.	kilowatt(s)

L

L.	In Roman numerals 50
lb.	A pound sterling
lb.	A pound weight
L/C	Letter of Credit.
Lib.	Library
Lim.	Limited
Lit.	Litre
Lght.	Length
log.	logarithm
Ltd.	Limited
ltd.	limited
lugg.	luggage

M

m.	Minute
m.	month

m.	metre
maj.	major
Mar.	March
max.	maximum
m/d	months after date
mads.	merchandise
med.	medium
m.m.	member
memo.	memorandum
Messrs.	Messieurs
mfg.	manufacturing
mfr.	manufacture
min.	minimum, minute
misc.	miscellaneous
M.M.	Messieures
m.m.	millimetre
M.O.	Money Order
m.o.	money order
Mon.	Monday
m.p.h.	mile per hour
Mr.	Mister
M/s.	Messers
Mrs.	Mistress/Misses
Ms.	Manuscript
MS.	Manuscript
ms.	manuscript
mfr.	manufacturer
m.g.	miligram
Mgr.	Manager
mgr.	manager
Mks.	marks
m/s	months after sight
mths.	months
mos.	months
mts.	minutes
Mtge.	mortgage

N

n	near
n.a.	no account, not applicable
N.B.	nota bene (mark well)
neg.	negative
nem con.	no one objecting
No.	number
no.	number
nom.cap	nominal capital
Nov.	November
nr.	near
n.s.	not specified

O

O.	Order
o.	order
o.a.	on account (of)
O/a.	on account (Of)
o.c.	overchange, office
O.C.	Office Copy
o.d.	on demand
o.s.	out of stock
%	per cent
oz.	ounce

P

p.	per or through
p.a.	per annum
pc.	per cent
pcl.	parcel
pd.	paid
per ann.	per annum
per pro.	per procuration; by proxy
p.m.	per month
P.N.	Promissory Note
P.O.	Postal Order
pp.	pages
P.P.	parcel Post
pro.	for
pro.tem.	for the time being
prox.	proximo, next
pkg.	packing
p. & L.	Profit and Loss
p.m.	post meridium (after noon)
pm.	premium, month
P.S.	postscript
P.T.O.	Please turn over
Petite	Vietesse (Ordinary goods train)

Q

q.v.	quod vide (which see)
qual.	quality.
qy.	query

R

Re.	Refer or referring to
re.	refer or referring to
recd.	received
recpt.	receipt
refce.	reference
regd.	registered
retd.	returned

retd.	retired
R.P.	reply paid
R.S.V.P.	repondex sil vous plait (please reply)

S

S.	Shilling
S/d.	Sight draft
Sec.	Secretary
se.	Secretary, second
senr.	Senior
sh.	shilling
S.N.	Shipping Note
Sq.	Square
Sq.ft.	Square foot
Sq.yd.	Square yard
Sr.	Senior
SS.	Steamship
S/S	Steamship
Stg.	Sterling
Str.	Steamer
Subs.cap.	subscribed, capital

T

T.L.O.	Total loss only
tgm.	telegram
tr.	tare (weight)

U

ult.	ultimo (last month)
UK	United Kingdom
USA	United States of Amercia

V

via.	by way of
V.P.L.	Valueable Payable Letter
V.P.P.	Value Payable Post
viz.	namely

W & Y

wt.	weight
yd.	yard
yr.	year

SEVENTEEN

WORDS COMMONLY CONFUSED

A, An

A is used before a word which starts with a constant sound while *An* is used before a word which starts with a vowel sound, e.g. *A* cashier, *An* Indian

According to, In accordance with

None of the two gives a direct expression and it is always desirable to write something natural. Thus instead of writing, *In accordance with* your request, it is better of write. 'We have the pleasure in sending a detailed folder that you requested for' etc.

Accept. Except

Accept means to receive or to confirm. *Except* means to omit.

Acknowledge, Acknowledging

Instead of writing 'We *acknowledge* with thanks the receipt of your letter, or 'while *acknowledging* your letter of ...' it is better to use a simple sentence like "Thank you for your letter of ..."

Affect, Effect

Affect means to influence. *Effect* (verb) means to cause or institute and *Effect* (noun) means a result.

All ready, Already

All ready means 'entirely' ready and *already* means 'by now' or 'by this time.

Alright, All right

It is always better to use the word 'All right.' *Alright* is wrong.

All together, Altogether

All together means all things or persons together while *altogether* means complete.

Among, Between

Among is always used when the objects are three or more. *Between* is used only when the objects are two.

Amount, Number

Amount refers to 'measurable quantity.' *Numbers* refers to 'countable quantity.'

And, Etc.

And should never be used with *Etc*. Thus 'table, chair, cot, almirah and *etc*.' is wrong. 'Table, chair, cot, almirah, *etc*.' is correct.

Anticipating

Always avoid using the word Anticipating. '*Anticipating* your order', or '*anticipating* your reply' is wrong.

Any place, Anywhere, Anywheres

Always use *anywhere* in place of any place or anywhere :

Appraise, Evaluate, Assess

Appraise and *evaluate* means to ascertain the value or amount of. *Assess* means to value for tax purposes.

Approve, Endorse

Approve means to sanction. *Endorse* means to have favourable opinion.

Apt, Likely, Liable

Apt denotes natural tendency, *likely* means probable. *Liable* means exposed to disadvantage or danger or legal responsibility.

As per

Use more natural expression. Thus instead of writing '*As per* your letter of . . .' it is better to write 'As you state in your letter.'

At, about

Always use *about*. Thus *at about* 5 p.m. is not correct while '*about* 5 p.m.' is correct.

Attached herewith

Anything attached is necessarily herewith. Say *attached* to this letter, not *attached herewith*.

Beg

It is too humble. As far as possible avoid its use.

Beside, Besides

Beside means along the side. *Besides* means 'in addition to' or 'with the exception of'.

Best of any

The expression should be 'best of those' of 'better than any other.'

Can, May

Can means capability. *May* means with permission.

Cannot help but

Note that the 'not' and the 'but' make a double negative. Omit but, thus say '*cannot help*.'

Can't, hardly

This is again a double negative. Use either '*can't*' or *hardly*'. Thus 'I can *hardly* see anything' or 'I can't'.

Cite, Sight, Site

Cite means to call attention to. *Sight* means something seen, and *site* is location.

Data

Data is a plural of datum.

Deal

Avoid it for representing to mean Bargain or Transaction.

Different than, Different from

The preferred idiom is *different from* and hence avoid using *different than.*

Due to

Due is a predicate adjective meaning due efficiency. Do not use '*due to*' in situations that can take 'because of' 'owing to'.

Farther, Further

Farther means distance. *Further* means to advance (degree).

Favour

Never call a letter a favour. Thus instead of writing 'please *favour* as with a reply 'write' please send us your reply.'

Fewer, Lesser

Fewer is used for 'Countable quantities' and *Lesser* is used for 'Measurable quantities'.

Former, Latter

These words should be used while referring to one of the two things or persons. In all other cases the correct usage is 'first and the last'.

Good, Well

Good is generally adjective while *well* is generally an adverb, e.g. He is a *good* boy ; he is getting on *well* with his studies.

Imply, infer

Imply means 'to express indirectly'. *Infer* means 'to deduce.'

Irregardless, Regardless

The use of *Irregardless* is incorrect. Always use *regardless.*

Kind of a, Sort of a

Avoid 'a' in both cases.

Leave, Let

Leave means to go away from : *Let* means 'to allow' e.g. '*Leave* me alone,' '*Let* me do my job.'

Might of, Must of

Never use these words. Instead use 'Might have : Must have.'

Most, All

Never use these two contradictory words. Always use '*Almost* all'.

Off, of

Never use *of* after *off*. Thus 'He hardly went *off* of the street' is incorrect. 'He hardly went *off* the street' is correct.

Oral, Verbal

Oral or written paper. 'As per verbal instruction' is correct usage.

Principal, Principle

Principal means head of an institution, organisation etc. *Principle* means fundamental rule.

Raise, Rise

Raise means to move up. 'His salary has been *raised*'. Rise means to move up. 'Prices of many commodities have *risen* up.'

Re

Abbreviation *re* for 'regarding should' always be avoided : Use regarding instead of *re.*

Reason is because, Reason is that

The correct usage is, *reason is that,* and not *reason in because.*

Recent date

Give the exact date instead of writing 'recent date'.

Same

Usage of *same* as a pronoun is incorrect.

Sit, Set

Sit means 'to be seated', *set* means 'to put in position'.

Stationary, stationery

Former means 'not moving,' latter means 'writing supplies.'

This there, That there

Do not use 'there' with 'this' or 'that'.

These kind

Since kind is singular *these* should not be used with it. The correct usuage therefore is *this kind.*

Thusly

It is an irritating word. Use '*thus*' only.

We, I

The word *we* is used when it is desired to represent a company or firm in business writting. However, when it is desired to represent or speak for an individual, use only *I.*

EIGHTEEN

WORDS COMMONLY MISSPELT

Corect spellings are important for accuracy, clarity and effective communication in business correspondence. Poor spellings are bound to create a very bad impression on the recipient. They will project a very damaging image of you and your business. English spellings are tricky and irritating if they are not paid proper attention. You have to be very particular about them. It has been an established fact that correct spellings in our business letters is a big dividend paying factor.

Your poor spellings have nothing to do with your business-skills, expertise or educational qualifications. What is required is a will and planned efforts to improve them. A readymade list of words often misspelled in business correspondence can go a long way to help you master your spellings. Below is give a list of such common words to help you over come your spelling problems

A

abatement

absence

absurd

abundance

abundant

accidentally

academy

accommodation

accompany

accomplish

accordance

accordingly

accountant

accustom
achieve
acknowledgement
adjourn
admiration
adventure
affect
affectionately
affidavit
agreement
alcohol
alloyed
all right
altogether
altogetherness
amateur
ambassador
admission
ambitious
ancestor
ancient
announce
annual
antiseptic
anywhere

apparatus
apparently
appearance
applause
appreciation
appropriation
approval
approved
approximately
architect
architectural
archives
arctic
area
areal
ascending
assemble
assign
assignment
assistance
assume
assuring
astonishing
athlete
attaching

attacked
attendance
attendant
attract
attraction
audience
auditor
available
average

B

baggage
balance
balcony
bankrupt
bankruptcy
banquet
barbarous
barley
basement
beautiful
begin
beginning
belief

believe
beneficial
beneficent
bestial
beverage
beware
book-keeper
bonded
boundary
bouquet
boycott
breadth
bridle
brilliant
brokerage
bronze
brought
bubbling
bucket
budgetary
buffet
bulletin
burden
bureau
bureaucracy
burglar
burial
business
butterfly

C

camera
campaign
cannon
canvas
canvass
capable
captive
career
cargoes
cathedral
cauliflower
cease
celebration
celibrity
cemetery
census
ceremony
challenge
champion
changeable
chemist
choir
Christmas
circular
circus
civilization
circumstances
claim
claimant
clothier
coalesce
coarse
cobbler
colonist
colony
column
combination
commandable
commission
committee
committed
communication
community

comparison
compass
compel
compelled
compensation
competition
compilation
completely
complexion
compositon
comprehend
comrade
conceal
concede
conclude
condemn
conference
confess
confidence
confusion
conscious
consequence
consequently
considerable
consolation
consult
contagious
contemptible
content
continual
continuous
contrary
controlled
controller
convenience
convention
convertible
cordial
cooperation
correspondence
corrupt
council
created
creature
credible
credibility
cricket
criminal
cripple
cruelty
cucumber
cultivate
cupboard
curious
current
cursory
cushion

D

deceive
decline
decrease
defence
deference
defy
degree
delicate
delicious
delight
delirious
delivery
deliverance
denial
dense

dependent
derision
deprive
depth
derive
descend
description
design
designate
desolate
despair
desperate
despised
destined
destruction
detective
development
device
devote
devour
diagnosis
dictate
dictator
difference
difficulty
dignity
dilemma
diphtheria
directory
disagreeable
disappear
disappointed
disapprove
disastrous
discontent
discount
discharge
discovery
disgrace
disguise
dismiss
disobey
disorder
dispensary
displeasure
dispose
dispute
dissent
dissolve
distinct
distinctive
distinguish
distress
disturb
divine
divisible
division
divorce
doctrine
doesn't
donkeys
doubtful
doubtless
draftsman
dreadful
drowned
drowsy
duplicate
dying

E

earthquake
echoes
economy

edited
editor
education
elated
electrician
electronics
elegant
elementary
elephant
elsewhere
emblem
embrace
emergency
emigrant
emperor
emphasize
encounter
encourage
endeavour
energy
engraver
enlarging
enormous
entertainment
entirely

entitle
equipped
equivalent
eraser
errand
especially
esteemed
estimate
eternal
ether
everyone
evidence
exaltation
exasperation
exceed
excel
excellent
exception
excess
excite
exclaim
exclamation
exlusive
execute
exhausted

exhibit
exhilarate
exiled
existence
exorbitant
expatriated
expedition
expelled
explain
explanation
exploit
explore
extravagance
exultation

F

faithfully
fallacious
familiar
famine
fascinate
fashion
favour
favourite

feasible
feature
February
feeble
feminist
fertile
fertilize
festival
fidelity
fiery
film
finance
financier
fission
fixture
flatter
favour
flourish
fluid
forcible
foremost
forfeit
forge
fortune
freight
frown
fruition
fulfil
fully
fundamental
furious
futility

G

galloping
gauge
generation
genius
gentleman
genuine
ghost
glamorous
glazier
glitter
glorious
glutton
goddess
goggles
gorgeous
gospel
government
graceful
gracious
gradual
grammar
grandeur
grateful
gratitude
greedy
grievance
groan
growth
guarantee
guardian
guess
guidance
guilty
guitar
gymnasium

H

handing
hardware

harmony
hasten
hatred
haughty
hazard
hearty
hedge
heir
henceforth
hereafter
hereby
heritage
herewith
heroic
hexagon
highway
hinderance
hippopotamus
hollow
honeyed
horizon
horrible
horror
household
hurriedly

hymn
hypen
hypocrisy

I

ideal
identification
identify
idol
ignorance
illiterate
imagination
immediately
immense
immoral
immunity
imperative
imperial
impression
inadequate
inauguration
inadequate
incline
inconvenience

indefinitely
indignation
individual
indivisible
induce
inevitable
inferior
infinite
inhabitant
initial
innoculation
inquiry
inspire
instance
instant
institution
instrument
itegration
intelligence
intercede
interior
intimate
invariable
invisible
invoice

iodine

irregular

irrelevant

irresistible

isthmus

items

ivory

J

jewelry/jewellery

judicial

jurisdiction

jury

justify

jute

juvenile

juxtapose

K

kangaroo

kerosene

keynote

khaki

kidnapped

kilometre

kindergarten

kinetic

kleptomania

knack

knapsack

knave

knead

knick-knack

knit

knock

knoll

knowledge

knowledgeable

kudos

L

labelled

laboratory

laborious

labyrinth

laconic

laggard

laity

lamentable

languid

langour

lapse

largess

larva

lassitude

latent

lateral

latitude

later

laudable

launch

laurel

lavish

laid

laying

leading

league

legend

legendary

legible

legislate

leisure

length

lenient
lens
leopard
lesson
lethal
lethargic
leverage
lewd
lexicon
liability
liaison
libel
lichen
lied
lien
lieu
lieutenant
likely
lineage
linguist
liquidate
liquor
litre
litigation
livelihood
liveliness
loan
loath
locale
longevity
longitude
loquacious
lucid
lucrative
luminary
lunar
lustre
lustrous
luxuriant
luxurious
lyre

M

machination
madam
maestro
magazine
magisterial
magnanimity
magnate
magnitude
maintain
maintenance
majestically
majority
malicious
malign
mail
mammoth
mandate
manifest
manifesto
manifold
manipulate
manufacture
marital
maritime
martial
martyr
marvellous
massacre
massage
material
mature

mausoleum
maxim
mean
mechanism
meddlesome
medical
medicinal
medicine
mediocre
meditation
medium
melancholy
memoir
memorandum
meningitis
menthol
mentor
menu
merely
merit
meteorology
migrant
milage
militant
millenium

miniature
minister
minutes
miracle
misapprehension
misconstrue
miscreant
misgiving
mishap
mishappen
misspell
mitigate
mobile
mobilize
moderate
momentous
monetary
monotonous
morbid
mortify
motivate
mountanous
mournful
muddle
multiplication

multiply
multiplicity
municipal
muscle
musician
mutilate
mutinous
mutual
myriad

N

naive
naptha
narrate
narration
nautical
naval
necessary
necessitate
negation
negligent
neither
nephew
nepotism

neurology
nicety
niche
nickel
nocturnal
nomenclature
nominal
non-committal
non-descript
nonentity
nostalgia
noticeable
notorious
novice
noxious
nuisance
numb
nuptial
nutrient

O

oasis
oath
obedience
obedient
obituary
obligatory
oblige
obliterate
oblivion
obnoxious
obsolete
obstacle
obstinate
obviate
occasion
occasional
occupy
occur
oceanic
odyssey
offensive
official
officious
often
omelette/omelet
ominous
omission
omnipotent
omnipresent
once
onslaught
opaque
operate
optimism
opponent
opportune
opportunity
oppose
opposite
option
oral
ordeal
ordinance
ordinary
organization
organizer
origin
ornate
orphan
oscillate
ostensible
ostentatious
ought

oust

outrageous

overt

oxidation

P

pacifist

pacify

pageant

palatable

palatial

palmist

palpable

paltry

panacea

pancreas

pandemonium

panic

panorma

parachute

parade

paradox

paradise

paraffin

paragraph

parallel

paralysis

paralyze

parcel

parity

parley

parliament

parochial

parry

partial

particle

particular

passive

pasteurize

pastime

pastoral

patent

patience

patrimony

patriot

patron

pattern

pavement

pavilion

pieceable

peacefully

peanut

pearly

peculiar

pedestal

penal

pencillin

penitence

penitent

penniless

pension

perceive

percentage

perfection

perfume

perish

perjury

permeate

permissible

permission

perpetual

persistence

personally

persuade

petition
phenomenon
philosophy
phrase
picknicking
pierced
pigeon
pilgrim
pillar
pineapple
pioneer
plague
plunge
pneumonia
poem
poetry
policy
politician
possess
possession
possibility
posterity
potatoes
pottery
poultry

poverty
practically
preach
preamble
precede
precious
preference
premises
preparation
prescribe
presence
preside
presume
previous
prey
primary
princess
principal
principle
privilege
proceed
procession
progression
prolong
prominent

prophecy
prophesy
prophet
proportion
proposition
prospect
prosperity
protein
province
provision
provoke
psychology
publication
punishment
pursue
purveyor
putrefy
puzzle
pyre

Q

quack
qualify
qualm

quantity
question
questionable
questionnaire
queue
quickly
quiet
quire
quirk
quite
quixotic
quiz
quizzical
quorum
quotation
quotient

R

rabid
racism
rainbow
rapture
rancour
random
ransack
rapacious
rapport
rarity
rational
ravage
raze
razor
reactionary
readily
realistic
reality
realization
realm
ream
reasonable
recede
receipt
receivable
recess
recession
recipe
recipient
reciprocal
reconize
reconcile
record
recrimination
recruit
rectify
rectitude
recur
redoubtable
redress
reducible
redundant
refer
referendum
reflex
refute
regal
regale
regarding
regardless
regime
regiment
register
registration
regular
rehersal

reign
reiterate
rejuvenate
relay
relegate
relevant
reliable
reliance
relief
relieve
religion
relinquish
reliable
remediable
remedial
remembrance
reminisce
reminiscence
remittance
remonstrate
render
rendezvous
renew
renovate
renown
renuniciation
reparation
repentance
repertory
repetition
repetitious
replenish
replete
reprehensible
reprieve
reprimand
reprobate
repudiate
repugnance
reputable
reputation
resemble
reservoir
residue
resign
resilient
resin
resolve
resource
respectable
repectively
resplendent
response
responsibility
restive
resume
resurgence
reticent
retina
retinue
retribution
retrieve
retrospective
revelation
reverberate
reverence
reverent
revocable
rhetoric
rhinoceros
ridiculous
righteous
rinse
rise
rising

rivalry
robot
robust
rogue
rosary
rostrum
rotate
rotund
rouge
rough
route
rubble
ruddy
rudiment
ruin
rumour
ruthless

S

sacred
sacrifice
sacrificial
sacrilege
saddle
sagacious
sagacity
salable
salacious
salient
saline
salubrious
salute
salvage
sample
sanctuary
sanguine
sanitary
sapphire
sarcasm
satellite
satisfaction
satisfactory
saturate
scarce
scarcity
scent
schedule
scholarship
science
scientist
secondary
secretary
secular
security
sedative
seduce
seize
seizure
semblance
sensible
sentinel
serenity
sergeant
serious
series
serpent
servile
several
settlement
sheaf
shepherd
shrewd
shriek
sigh

sign
similar
simile
sincerely
site
situated
skeptic
skilful
slippery
slothful
slough
sluice
smug
snatch
sojourn
solace
soldier
solemn
solitary
solitude
solve
solvent
somewhat
somewhere
sonorous
source
souvenir
sovereign
spangle
spate
spatial
speak
speciality
specified
spectacle
spectacular
spectator
sphere
sphinx
spirits
splendour
sprinkle
spurious
squash
squirrel
stable
stabilize
stagger
stagnant
staid
stake
starch
stare
stately
static
stationary
statue
steeple
stethoscope
stitch
strait
strategic
strawberry
strengthen
stubborn
studious
stuble
subdued
substance
successful
sufficient
suggestion
suitable
superficial
superintendent

supervisor
surrender
sorround
surveyed
sustain
symbol
symmetry
sympathy
syrup

T

tableau
tactics
tailor
tangible
tannery
telepathy
temperate
temperature
tempest
temporary
temptation
terrestrial
testimony
textile
thermometer
thirsty
thrice
throne
torment
tornado
tortoise
torture
tortuous
toxic
tradition
tragedy
traitor
trample
translate
transportation
tread
treasury
tremble
trespassing
tributary
trifle
triumph
trumpet
tuberclosis
turtle
twilight
twinkle
typewriter
tyranny
tyrant

U

ubiquitous
umbrella
uncertain
uncle
uncivilized
unconscious
uncontrollable
underneath
undoubtedly
uneasy
unexpected
unforgettable
unfortunately
unintelligible
unmanageable

unmitigated
unnecessary
unparalleled
unprecedented
until
unusual
unwieldy
upbraid
upright
urban
urbane
usable
usage
usually
usurer
usurp
utility
utilize
utmost
utterance

V

vacancy
vacate
vaccinate
vaccine
vacuum
vagary
vagarant
valedictory
valid
vanity
vault
vehement
vehicle
veil
velvet
venerable
vengeance
ventilate
venture
verse
via
viceroy
victim
victorious
videotape
view
vigilant
vilify
villain
vindicate
vindictive
violence
virgin
virile
virtue
virtuous
vivacious
vogue
volatile
voluntary
votary
vulcanize
vulnerable
vulgar
vulture

W

waive
waiver
wander
warrant

wear
weather
where
whereby
wherefore
wherein
whirl
whistle
whimsical
whoever
whole
wholesome
width
wield
wilderness
wintry
witch
wither
withhold
woeful
womanfolk
wondrous
woo
worshipped
worsted
wrack
wrap
wrath
wreath
wrench
wrest
wrestle
wretched
wriggle
wrinkle
wrist
write
wrong

X

xenophobia
xylophone

Y

yacht
yea
yeoman
yield
yoghurt
yours
yourself
youth
youthful

Z

zealot
zealous
zenith
zephyr
zodiac
zoology

OUR PUBLICATIONS

ENGLISH IMPROVEMENT

G-1	Secondary School Grammar and Composition	55.00
G-2	3000 Words for Better Vocabulary	30.00
G-5	Spelling Power Made Easy	30.00
G-7	3000 Synonyms & Antonyms	30.00
G-8	3000 Idioms & Phrases	30.00
G-9	3000 Quotations	30.00
G-10	3000 Proverbs	30.00
G-11	3000 Common Errors in English	30.00
G-19	Dictionary of Idioms & Phrases	55.00
G-25	Dictionary of Quotations	40.00
G-26	Improve Your English	30.00
G-28	Improve Your Vocabulary	30.00
G-29	Dictionary of Synonyms & Antonyms	45.00
G-33	Common Errors in English	30.00
G-34	Improve Your Idioms & Phrases	30.00
G-41	Basic English Grammar for Schools	30.00
G-45	Dictionary for Proverbs	40.00

ESSAY WRITING

G-3	Up-to-date School Essays, Letters and Stories	30.00
G-17	School Essays, Letters & Paragraphs	22.00
G-18	School Essays, Letters for Juniors	22.00
G-30	Selected Essays	35.00
G-31	Latest Essays	55.00
G-32	160 Essays	90.00

LETTER WRITING

G-6	Stolen Love Letters	25.00
G-20	Readymade Letters	30.00
G-38	Improve Your Business Letters	40.00
G-39	How to Write Effective Business Letters	40.00
G-40	Readymade Business Letters	40.00
G-42	Standard Book of Moral Letters	30.00
G-44	Lively Love Letters	30.00
G-47	How to Write Impressive Business Letters	55.00
G-48	Top Winning Letters	35.00

I.Q. AND INTELLIGENCE

G-16	Test Your I.Q.	30.00
G-22	Check Your I.Q.	28.00
G-23	How to Improve Your I.Q.	28.00
G-24	I.Q. for All	28.00
G-27	Better Your I.Q.	28.00

JOKES

G-12	Top Party Jokes	25.00
G-13	1001 Jokes	25.00
G-14	Bachelors' Jokes	25.00
G-15	Childrens' Jokes	22.00
G-21	Lovers' Jokes	25.00

MISCELLANEOUS

G-4	How to Pass Exams	30.00
G-35	G.K. Quiz	30.00
G-36	Improve Your Eyesight	35.00
G-37	The Book of Etiquette	35.00
G-43	Prophet-Kahlil Gibran	25.00
G-46	The Book of Baby Names	30.00